AMERICAN LABOR AND
THE INDOCHINA WAR

D0815035

AMONG BOOKS BY THE SAME AUTHOR

The Life and Writings of Frederick Douglass (4 vols.)
History of the Labor Movement in the United States (4 vols.)
A History of Cuba and Its Relations with the United States (2 vols.)
Business and Slavery: The New York Merchants and the Irrepressible Conflict
The Fur and Leather Workers Union
Jack London: American Rebel
Mark Twain: Social Critic
The Jews in American History: 1654–1865
The Autobiographies of the Haymarket Martyrs
The Case of Joe Hill
The Letters of Joe Hill
The Bolshevik Revolution: Its Impact on American Radicals, Liberals, and Labor
The Black Panthers Speak
W.E.B. Du Bois Speaks (2 vols.)
Helen Keller: Her Socialist Years

American Labor and the Indochina War

The Growth of Union Opposition

by PHILIP S. FONER

INTERNATIONAL PUBLISHERS
New York

Copyright © by International Publishers Co., Inc., 1971

ALL RIGHTS RESERVED

First Edition, 1971

Library of Congress Catalog Card Number: 70–152909

SBN 7178–0323–6

Printed in the United States of America

CONTENTS

We've had it!

We the undersigned Bay Area trade union officers, executive board members and shop stewards have sent the following message to President Richard M. Nixon with a copy to Senate Foreign Relations Committee Chairman J. William Fulbright:

Dear Mr. President:

American working people and their families are deeply disturbed at your expansion of the war into Cambodia. Those men being killed are our sons — new casualty lists to add to the 40,000 already dead and 300,000 wounded in Vietnam.

On April 20 you announced that 150,000 men would be removed within the course of a year. Although we felt that even that pace was too slow, we hoped this was a turn toward peace, an end to the killing.

Now you have further divided this country by a number of blatant reversals in the course of a few days. First there were arms to Cambodia. Then there were American "advisors." Now an invasion in force!

This took place without even the pretext of a request from Cambodia, which international law considers a neutral nation.

This is a direct break with the US Constitution. Only Congress can declare war. Furthermore, you did not even consult with the Senate Foreign Relations Committee— the committee mainly responsible to advise and consent. Your own Secretary of State William P. Rogers testified he told Congress that the United States would not escalate the war into Cambodia. Little wonder there are members of your own party who have said you have "broken faith with Congress."

You have created a credibility gap of incredible proportions.

You have pledged to the American people that we will be out of Cambodia by June 30.

In the light of this record, all we can say is — we don't believe you!

The economy of our country is steadily being eroded; your promises to stabilize the economy and control inflation have become meaningless. Our paychecks buy less for our families; our standard of living has been assaulted. We are suffering increased inflation and unemployment.

Now Cambodia! What next?

There must be an end to these military adventures.

We want a cease-fire — Now!
We want out of Cambodia — Now!
We want out of Vietnam — Now!
We've had it!

Most important, this nation of ours must turn from war to peace. Any other course leads to disaster.

From a full-page advertisement in the San Francisco Chronicle, May 18, 1970, in the form of an open letter to the President. It was signed by over 450 trade union officials, executive board members and shop stewards in the Bay Area.

1

INTRODUCTION

THE SPEAKER WAS DR. MARTIN LUTHER KING, JR., BLACK CIVIL RIGHTS LEADER AND NOBEL PEACE PRIZE winner. The setting was the handsome headquarters of the Council for Continuing Education on the campus of the University of Chicago. The date was November 27, 1967. The occasion was the National Labor Leadership Assembly for Peace. The audience was composed of 523 leaders from 50 international unions in 38 states and hundreds of local unions across the country. Said Dr. King:

Tens of thousands of Americans oppose the war in Vietnam. Never before in our history has there been such a passionate and enormous popular resistance to a current war.

But one voice was missing—the loud, clear voice of labor. The absence of that one voice was all the more tragic because it may be the decisive one for tipping the balance towards peace.[1]

In order to understand why that voice was missing one must go back in our history over half a century before the United States became involved in the "dirty war" in Southeast Asia.

It will come as a surprise to many even inside the labor movement to learn that organized labor was an important force in the first anti-imperialist movement in American history. When, during the Spanish-American War, it became clear that the war launched supposedly to liberate Cuba was in actuality a brutal colonial war of conquest against the Cuban, Puerto Rican, and especially the Filipino people, many Americans joined in voicing opposition to the policy of military conquest. With few exceptions the labor movement joined the ranks of the anti-imperialists. Some trade unionists did so because they were concerned about an influx of cheap labor from Asian colonies as a threat to workers' living standards. Others were not opposed to the expansion of U.S. commerce, power, and influence, but vigorously rejected the concept of territorial annexation and the military conquest of people to be ruled without their consent. They saw, too, that imperialism abroad would strengthen the power of anti-labor monopolies at home. At its conventions in 1898 and 1899, the American Federation of Labor adopted resolutions emphasizing that the oppressors of the colonial people were also the oppressors of the working class of the United States, and that imperialism would lead only to further repression of the American labor movement.[2]

After 1900 anti-imperialist activity within the labor movement receded. Indeed, many labor leaders came to accept the idea that progress by unions at home was dependent on capitalism and the expansion of American corporations abroad. Furthermore, as Lenin pointed out in his study of imperialist development, imperialism tended "to create privileged ranks among the workers and to separate them from the broad mass of the proletariat." Just as the British imperialists were able to blunt the anti-imperialist sentiments of organized labor in England by corrupting the skilled workers, giving them a share in the spoils from the exploitation of colonies, so American imperialists succeeded in achieving this in the United States, even though the American form of imperialism operated less through outright possession of colonies and more through indirect domination or, to use a more contemporary expression, through neo-colonialism.[3]

Yet the earlier anti-imperialist tradition of the American working class was never completely destroyed. It found expression in the opposition in labor circles to militarism and war. There was considerable labor opposition to President Woodrow Wilson's armed intervention in Mexico during the summer of 1916, and many trade unions denounced the intervention on the ground that it was aimed at "crushing the ideals and hopes of the Mexican laboring people."[4]

When World War I broke out in 1914, the majority of the trade unions and the AFL itself condemned the war and called for its end. But by the fall of 1916 Samuel Gompers, AFL President, was insisting that organized labor had to endorse the idea of the United States joining the crusade against the Kaiser's autocracy. Determined to place the AFL on record behind the Wilson Administration as it moved toward war and to brook no opposition from the strong opponents of war in trade union ranks, Gompers called a conference in February 1917 of all affiliated unions. Gompers and his associates ran roughshod over all present at the conference who voiced labor's opposition to the war. They rammed through a statement affirming that should the United States be drawn into the European conflict, the AFL would "offer our services to our country in every field of activity to defend, safeguard and preserve the Republic of the United States of America against its enemies."[5]

The AFL leadership also became involved in implementing President Wilson's program toward Russia after the February revolution in 1917 had ousted the Tsar. The AFL leadership worked to bolster Kerensky's government and keep it in the war, and even more energetically after the successful Bolshevik Revolution, to aid the Wilsonian campaign to overthrow the Bolsheviks, including armed intervention in behalf of the counter-revolutionists.

But large and important sections of the American labor movement enthusiastically supported the Bolshevik Revolution, and bitterly opposed Wilson's interventionist policy against the young Soviet Republic as well as the role played by the top AFL leaders. At the 1919 and 1920 AFL conventions resolutions were introduced calling for recognition of Soviet Russia by the United States, for lifting the Allied blockade on Russian ports so that food and clothing might reach the Russian people, for the withdrawal of American troops from Russia leaving the Russian people "to regulate their own affairs."[6] In addition, many international and local unions, city centrals and state federations of labor rallied to the support of the embattled Russian workers and peasants and opposed intervention against Russia through speeches and resolutions.

The close relationship between the AFL leadership and the government in foreign policy matters established during World War I continued during the 1920's and 1930's. When many Americans, including a number of trade unions, condemned the U.S. military intervention against Sandino in Nicaragua in 1927, the AFL endorsed it as necessary to keep Latin America free of "communist subversion." Throughout the twenties and into the thirties, the AFL leadership continued its bitter opposition to American recognition of Soviet Russia, and when President Franklin D. Roosevelt on November 16, 1933 finally established diplomatic relations between the United States and the Soviet Union, the AFL Executive Council denounced the action as "a betrayal of the American people."[7]

With the birth of the CIO in 1935, new and large sections of the labor movement asserted themselves in a progressive manner in the field of foreign policy. A number of unions which came into existence during the drive to organize the mass production industries as well as those which had been expelled from the AFL for leading the organizing campaign, condemned fascism and war. They supported the fight of the Spanish Republic against Hitler-backed Franco, boycotted Japanese and German products, and supported anti-fascists in every struggle. The CIO endorsed this policy at its national convention in 1937 and also gave approval of the call issued by President Roosevelt in that year urging the nations of the world to "quarantine the aggressors."

In 1938 the CIO supported Mexican President Cardenas' expropriation of British and American oil companies while the AFL leaders condemned it as interference with private property and supported Secretary of State Cordell Hull's demand for immediate compensation for expropriated American property. When the

Confederation of Latin American Workers (CTAL), founded by progressive and left-wing trade unionists in Latin America, held its first general Congress in Mexico City, November 1941, a large fraternal delegation was present from the CIO, and greetings of solidarity were sent to the Congress by Philip Murray, CIO president.

These events indicated that an important section of the American labor movement was speaking with a new voice in foreign affairs. In the years immediately following World War II, this voice continued to be heard. At its 1947 convention the CIO's foreign policy resolution demanded a policy of peace, opposed fascism, urged destruction of all atomic bombs, supported the independence struggle of colonial peoples, and emphasized the need for fraternal relations with the Soviet Union and close collaboration between the labor movements of the United States and the All-Union Central Council of Trade Unions of the Soviet Union. The CIO was allied with the Soviet trade unions in the World Federation of Trade Unions formed at the close of the Second World War by the trade union centers of the Allied and liberated nations.[8]

Yet soon enough the leaders of the CIO were supporting the main foreign policy program of big business in the United States. After V-J Day, President Truman scuttled the policies of his predecessor for peaceful and friendly coexistence with the Soviet Union and embarked on the cold war. As the cold war intensified, the State Department and other government agencies called upon the trade union movement for cooperation. Within a few years, not only did the CIO join in partnership with the AFL in supporting the cold-war policy of the Truman Administration; it copied the AFL by sending representatives on missions to split the trade unions in European countries and weaken the opposition abroad to U.S. foreign policy. The State Department appointed labor representatives of both AFL and CIO to the staffs of various American embassies and foreign missions. These "striped pants" labor diplomats were regarded as essential for the success of cold-war policies since they had access to labor gatherings where the usual diplomats would be unwelcome. It was, as Harry Bridges aptly put it, "American imperialism with a union label."

In 1949 Murray withdrew the CIO from the World Federation of Trade Unions, an action taken without even consulting his Executive Board. Then, again without consulting the Board, the CIO leaders joined with the AFL to set up the International Confederation of Free Trade Unions to split the WFTU. The sole guiding principle of the new international body was anti-communism.[9]

At the eleventh CIO convention in 1949 the process of tieing the organization to the cold war was completed. The Constitution Committee proposed a catch-all resolution that would bar anyone from the CIO's Executive Board who followed "policies and activities directed toward the achievement or purposes of the Communist Party." Then followed a resolution to expel the 50,000-strong United Electrical, Radio and Machine Workers of America because it did not support the Marshall Plan or the North Atlantic Pact, and had endorsed Henry Wallace, candidate for President in 1948 of the Progressive Party whose platform favored a return to the policies of Franklin D. Roosevelt at home and abroad. Without a trial or hearing, the expulsion was voted, and the charter of the electrical workers handed to James B. Carey, the leading CIO cold-war advocate and acknowledged agent of the then reactionary Association of Catholic Trade Unionists. The next day, the Farm Equipment Workers were expelled and the union's jurisdiction turned over to the United Auto Workers. In all, eleven progressive unions were expelled by the CIO.[10]

While this shameful procedure was under way, Carey, one of the chief architects of the expulsion, spoke in his capacity as CIO secretary-treasurer to an American Legion-sponsored "anti-Communist" conference in New York City. He told the leaders of the military, government and big business gathered at the Astor Hotel: "In the last war we joined the Communists to fight the fascists; in another war we will join the fascists to fight the Communists."[11] Unity with fascists! Such was the trail's end of the new road taken by the leaders of the CIO. Now both wings of the organized labor movement spoke with one voice in foreign policy—the voice of the cold war!

In the late spring of 1953 the Executive Board of the United Packinghouse Workers of America examined the role labor had played in this period and decided that there must be "a very quick and drastic change in the thinking and action of the labor movement." In a statement entitled, "The Road Ahead," the UPW declared that discussions of peace, foreign affairs, war preparations, and social and economic questions had been "stifled," while spokesmen for big business had been unhampered in their drive for profits, markets abroad, and suppression of protest at home. "And with labor silent—and sometimes in agreement—big business has driven far toward these objectives. It is vital that labor re-examine its role before it is too late and reassert its fundamental right, perform its fundamental duty, to promote and insist upon the fullest discussions of these issues so vital to our very life." The UPW courageously called for

An end to the dictatorship of fear; an end to thought suppression; an end to repression by legislative investigation; fearless defense of every constitutional right of every person, popular or unpopular, regardless of race, color, creed or political belief; against every form of attack whether by criminal prosecution or by economic or social prosecution, whether by threat of jail or by threat of discharge; there must be a recognition that we need not fear free speech, even for Communists, but that we must fear suppression of speech even of Communists.

The UPW went on to point out that the capitulation of the labor movement to the witchhunters was a direct consequence of its support of the cold war policy. The union appealed for a reversal of uncritical support of the foreign policy of the United States by organized labor.

After two decades of bitter rivalry, serious negotiations got under way in 1955 for the merger of the two American labor federations. *The Nation* appealed on December 10, 1955 to the negotiating committee to heed the growing demand for an end to the cold war voiced by many Americans, including some even in the labor movement, who had become aware that their government's foreign policy, if not reversed, would lead inevitably to a thermonuclear war which would destroy all mankind. "The millions who are in search of peace," it pleaded, "have the right to look to the ranks of labor for support—and perhaps for leadership. Whether that challenge is met will depend on whether the drive toward peace, undeniably widespread through the rank and file of the labor movement, can break through the crust of a top-level policy which sees 'containment' and 'liberation' as more desirable goals than peaceful coexistence."[12]

It was a vain hope. A number of AFL and CIO officials who had expressed concern over America's foreign policy and had publicly voiced a demand for peaceful relations with the Soviet Union, were members of the committees working out the AFL-CIO merger agreement. But they were utterly silent on the question of a new approach by organized labor in foreign policy once the merger became a reality. There was, to be sure, a battle over which organization should gain the chairmanship of the International Affairs Committee, and it was finally decided to have two at the helm: Jacob Potofsky of the Amalgamated Clothing Workers, representing the CIO, and Matthew Woll, the AFL's veteran and most bitter anti-communist, spokesmen for the Federation. But this arrangement only lasted two years: Potofsky resigned and Woll died. George Meany, president of the AFL-CIO, took the chairmanship for himself, but then relinquished it, first to George Harrison and, then, to George T. Brown, who shared his cold-war outlook. In actual fact, the International Affairs Department was run by the notorious Jay Lovestone, who had been serving as Meany's foreign affairs adviser for several years; his dominance over the Department was recognized officially by his appointment, first, as associated director, and, in 1963, as director. Both in his unofficial and official capacities, Lovestone continued his work as an ally of the State Department to rally the trade unions of

Europe, Latin America, Asia and Africa behind American leadership in the cold war against the "Russian threat."[13]

Before the merger both the AFL and CIO had supported the cold war and both had employed McCarthyite tactics against the opponents of this policy. The combined organization continued proudly to uphold the banner of anti-communism, and behind this patriotic shield, the most sordid transaction in the history of the American labor movement occurred. On May 22, 1966, Victor Reuther, international affairs director of the UAW, charged that the AFL-CIO's Department on International Affairs, headed by Jay Lovestone, was "involved" with the Central Intelligence Agency (CIA), and that the AFL-CIO and some of its affiliates "have permitted themselves to be used by the Central Intelligence Agency as a cover for clandestine operations abroad."[14]

Much of this was already common knowledge to readers of various publications,[15] but in the next few years, newspapers, magazines, and books spelled out the full details of how the AFL-CIO, under the Meany-Lovestone aegis, and with the assistance of Irving Brown as European trouble-shooter and Serafino Romualdi, as the main Lovestone-CIA agent in Latin America, fronted for the CIA in helping paid conservative unions in France, Italy, Greece, Germany, Latin America, Africa, and Asia fight the radicals and turn many of the unions into cold-war oriented organizations. They spelled out, too, the specific involvements of the Meany-Lovestone-CIA axis in the defeat of progressive and reform governments in the Dominican Republic, Guatemala, and British Guiana, and their longtime support of Batista in Cuba as well as their repeated efforts to overthrow the Revolutionary Government headed by Fidel Castro after the ouster of the hated Cuban dictator.[16]

These exposures of the AFL-CIO relations to the CIA occurred at a time when the United States was deeply involved in the war in Vietnam, and they helped both to explain in no small measure the enthusiastic support for the war in Southeast Asia by the AFL-CIO leadership and to stimulate the trend already under way in a number of AFL-CIO unions toward a policy calling for an end to the immoral, illegal and unconstitutional war.

The Vietnamese people have fought for their independence for at least a thousand years. They repelled the Chinese invasions for many centuries, and they conducted a heroic struggle against French colonial occupation of their country. French rule was broken by the Japanese who occupied Indochina during World War II. Nationalists, communists and socialists united in the Viet Minh, under the leadership of the Communist Ho Chi Minh, and fought in the interests of the anti-fascist alliance against the Japanese.

In September 1945, the Viet Minh established the Republic of Vietnam and proclaimed its independence from all colonial rule. (The Constitution of the Republic of Vietnam incorporated the famous principle set forth in the American Declaration of Independence, proclaiming the "self-evident" truths that "all men are created equal," and were endowed with "certain inalienable rights; that among these are life, liberty, and the pursuit of happiness.") Under an agreement signed in March 1946, the French recognized the Republic of Vietnam as "a free state, having its own government, parliament, army, and treasury, belonging to the Indochinese Federation and the French Union."

The Vietnamese people believed that this agreement settled the issue of colonialism once and for all. However, the French, determined to re-establish domination over an area so rich in resources, moved to reoccupy Indochina. The United States massively supported French efforts to block Indochinese independence and to impose a puppet regime on the people. The French also obtained the support of elements within Vietnam who became the allies of France against the independence struggle of their own people. One of the outstanding examples of such an ally of the French imperialists was Nguyen Cao Ky, Vice President of the present government in Saigon, a man whose attitude toward popular government is indicated by his statement, "My hero is Adolf Hitler."

The Geneva Conference of 1954 ended the war between France and the Republic of Vietnam. Vietnam was divided into two sections, the dividing line being the 17th parallel. However, it was recognized that Vietnam was one country, and it was agreed that in 1956 elections would be held in both North and South to determine the composition of a single government for the united nation. The United States, although present at the Geneva Conference, refused to sign the final agreement. However, it did agree that it would "refrain from use of force to upset the agreement."

While the United States could not stop the Geneva Agreement, it began immediately to undermine it. The French colonialists had not yet completed their withdrawal from Saigon when America's first para-military legions began arriving to support the South Vietnamese anti-Communist government of Ngo Dinh Diem. With the backing of the United States, Diem launched unbridled repression against all opposition forces and refused to allow the people of South Vietnam to vote in the elections scheduled for 1956. The reason was clear to all. As Eisenhower later conceded, "possibly 80 per cent of the population would have voted for the Communist Ho Chi Minh."

Basically the war in Vietnam began as a civil war. As Senator Frank Church pointed out in the *Saturday Evening Post* of April 24, 1965: "We only deceive ourselves when we pretend that the struggle in Vietnam is not a civil war. The two different parts of Vietnam don't represent two different peoples, with separate identities. Vietnam is a partitioned country in the grip of a continuing revolution."

But even this has changed with American intervention. "Every soldier, whatever he had been told before he arrived in South Vietnam," declared *The New Yorker* on January 23, 1971, "learned from bitter personal experience that he was engaged in a war against the South

Vietnamese people. . . . The problem (for the United States) in South Vietnam is not the traditional village system, or flaws in the pacification program, or even the Vietcong or the North Vietnamese. The problem is the South Vietnamese themselves."

As the Eisenhower Administration drew to a close, the Diem government, despite large-scale military aid from the United States, was falling apart. Powerful forces in this country tried to convince Eisenhower to send American troops to save Diem, but the President, convinced that the United States could not win a land war in Asia, had resisted the pressure to the end of his term in office.

2

LABOR BEGINS TO MOVE

IN HIS FAREWELL ADDRESS OF JANUARY 17, 1961, PRESIDENT DWIGHT D. EISENHOWER ISSUED A TIMELY AND portentous warning to the American people. "We must," he said, "guard against the acquisition of unwarranted influence, whether sought or unsought, by this military-industrial complex. This conjunction of an immense military establishment with a large arms industry is new in American experience. Its total influence—economic, political, even spiritual—is felt in every city, every statehouse, every office of federal government."[1] No warning by an American President was ever more authentic. A large segment of business, labor, the scientific and engineering communities, and the universities were all being generously subsidized from the $50 billion a year military budget. Defense orders placed in many communities were tieing their populations to the warfare state.

The "Juggernaut," as Fred Cook described the military-industrial complex,[2] rolled on during the Kennedy Administration, and along with it American involvement in the civil war in Vietnam increased. Under Kennedy, American military advisers were sent to South Vietnam and increased steadily to 15,500 men. After Kennedy's assassination, President Johnson escalated the war by augmenting American military forces in Vietnam and sending American jet bombers to destroy large parts of South Vietnam, killing and maiming thousands of civilians in the process. In the first days of August 1968, Johnson ordered the bombing of North Vietnam, and on the basis of the Tonkin Resolution, jammed through an intimidated Senate, the President, immediately after his election in November, began systematic, ruthless bombing of North Vietnam.[3]

The intensification of the bombing of North Vietnam to the point where more bombs were dropped on that small country than on Germany in all of World War II, the rise of U.S. military activity in South Vietnam to the deployment of a half-million-man army, and the increase in expenditures for carrying on the war to 30 billion dollars a year, are too familiar to need repeating. Less familiar, perhaps, is the history of the protest movement against the war in the United States and especially the gradual involvement of more and more sections of organized labor in this movement.

The bombing of North Vietnam was the turning point of the Vietnam war for many Americans. There had been protest against escalation before, but it had been scattered and largely confined to editorials in the radical and liberal press, a few speeches, and letters on the editorial pages of leading newspapers. The major concern in the late fifties and early sixties was with the civil rights movement. In the area of foreign affairs the attention of most Americans, including liberals and radicals, was riveted on the relations between the United States and the Cuban Revolution, dramatized by the CIA-sponsored Bay of Pigs invasion of April, 1961, and the overshadowing Cuban missile crisis. So far as the labor movement was concerned, Vietnam hardly figured in the proceedings of union conventions or in the labor press. In July 1964, President Leon J. Davis of Local 1199, Drug and Hospital Employees Union, Retail, Wholesale, and Department Store Union, AFL-CIO, warned of "the aggressive and dangerous foreign policy we are pursuing in Vietnam." But his was a solitary voice, and it was drowned out by George Meany's support of every step of escalation and his exhortations "for speedier and more thoroughgoing action to defeat the Viet Cong."[4]

The truth is that large sections of the labor movement saw the war as a solution to the pressing problem for which the unions had no other remedy. The period 1960–62, in which Americans were sent in increasing numbers to fight in Vietnam, coincided with a recovery from the recession of 1957–59. But while output of goods and services rose rapidly and profits soared, reaching record heights for peacetime (there was no declaration of war in Vietnam), employment lagged far behind productivity. Moreover, with machines doing much more of men's work, the task of finding jobs in the era of automation became a major concern of the labor movement. A feature article in the AFL-CIO *American Federationist* of October 1962 was entitled "The Specter of Rising Unemployment." It emphasized that "the economy of the United States has not been generating the number of jobs needed to meet the nation's requirements. The labor force is growing and increased productivity makes possible greater output with less labor."[5]

The remedy offered by most unions was simple: shorter hours and more defense spending. As the Vietnam war escalated, loading corporations with orders for the war, the demand for shorter hours was dropped—overtime was clearly now on the agenda—and the serious problem of lack of jobs, except for blacks, disappeared. Thus early in the history of American involvement in Vietnam, the workers, organized and unorganized, obtained a clear dollars-and-cents stake in supporting continuation of the war. Guns brought jobs, which brought butter to many hitherto unemployed or underemployed and lulled them into support of, or at least indifference to, a war without which, it appeared, they would return to the ranks of the unemployed.

Still, even at the very beginning of American involvement in the war there were some voices warning workers that they might be losing more than they gained from a war economy. Testifying before a House subcommittee in October 1962, William H. Ryan of the International Machinists Union expressed the feeling of many machinists who had found that government defense contracts subjected them to the whims of the Pentagon and that there was more reliability in civilian employment than in jobs tied to war production. "We have often wondered," Ryan declared, "if at the very bottom of the vicious influence working against peace is the profit motive of private munitions and armament manufacturers."[6]

But most observers were convinced that these words were wasted. Many workers remembered that as recently as World War II, arms buying by Britain and France helped pull the United States out of a depression that had resisted large doses of civilian pump-priming during the New Deal, and the post-World War II depression, until the outbreak of the Korean War, confirmed the argument that in our society wars provided employment. The *Wall Street Journal* put it succinctly on September 21, 1970: "Full employment, with the unemployment rate under 4%, for this country at least has been a phenomenon of war periods. We had it in World War II. We had it with the Korean War. And we had it with the Vietnam conflict prior to the recent throttling down of defense expenditure. But these are the only times we have had it."

Small wonder the "full dinner pail" argument was more influential than the dangers inherent in the military-industrial complex. To workers it appeared that the billions poured into war industries meant millions of jobs. The war was far away and jobs were a reality. After all, it did not require a Ph.D. in economics to figure out that when total defense expenditures at the height of World War II were in excess of 40 per cent of the gross national product, and 13.5 per cent at the height of the Korean War, and 9 per cent at the height of the Vietnam War, a good many jobs in this country were tied in with war production.[7]

Not until it became clear that the workers were getting "a progressively decreasing share of the swag" would labor leaders begin to speak out against the Vietnamese war in any considerable number. And not until it became clear that the war in Indochina lay at the root of the inflation that was eating away at the living standards of American workers and was even bringing rising unemployment with a decreasing number of workers riding on the defense gravy train, would opposition to the war become widespread among labor leaders and the trade unions. Even then unions which joined the anti-war movement had to conduct a persistent education to dispel the illusion among their members who opposed the war that it was unwise to speak out against its escalation because the war was creating prosperity. If this means that the moral aspects of the immoral war played a less significant role in sparking anti-war activity in the labor movement than did the economic facts of life, it might be remembered that the great upsurge of student opposition to the war coincided with increases in the draft.

The real beginning of organized protest against American involvement in Vietnam and the progressive enlargement of the war dates from March 24, 1965, when the first teach-in took place, at the University of Michigan. (Sit-in strikes of the thirties and sit-ins of the civil rights movement of the fifties were the ancestors of the teach-ins.) That night three experts on Vietnam—John Donahue of Michigan State, Robert Browne of Fairleigh Dickinson, and Arthur Waskow of the Institute of Policy Studies in Washington, D.C.—led the discussion. They were followed by two professors from the University of Michigan, after which some 30 professors led seminars till dawn. The attendance—2,800 students and faculty—surpassed the expectations of the organizers. The teach-in concluded with an outdoor rally at 8 a.m.

The idea spread quickly. Forty universities across the country sent telegrams of support, and sympathy demonstrations were held on the evening of the Michigan teach-in at the University of California at Berkeley and San Francisco State College. The teach-in movement, somewhat to the amazement of its organizers, spread not only to hundreds of American campuses but to England, Australia, Japan, even to South Vietnam. On May 15, 1965, a national teach-in in Washington featured a debate on Vietnam between defenders and opponents of American policy (Assistant Secretary of State McGeorge Bundy refused to participate) which was relayed to 110 campuses in 35 states and a nationwide home audience through TV and radio. On the same day, teach-ins were held at some 100 colleges and universities. On May 24, *Newsweek* commented that the teach-in had "evolved into an unprecedented phenomenon."

The teach-ins were based on the assumption that the government must be persuaded by a combination of argument and orderly demonstration to end the war by negotiating a settlement with the North Vietnamese and the National Liberation Front. Most of those involved were of the belief that the American presence in Vietnam was an accident and had no precedent in our history. They saw no connection between the war in Vietnam and the cold war or American foreign policy in general.[8] But as they developed, the teach-ins inevitably went beyond the scope set by the sponsors and opened up discussions of the 20-year-old cold war and the history and nature of American imperialism. During these discussions, more and more participants came to see that American atrocities in Vietnam were not chance violence, but part and parcel of a racist imperialist policy. In any case, whatever their limitations, the teach-ins made a most important contribution to the peace movement. As *The Nation* correctly observed: "The feeling of helplessness in the face of the war juggernaut is gone."[9]

1965 also saw the beginning of protest demonstrations off campuses, notably the first national mobilization against the war—the March on Washington to End the War on April 17, 1965, sponsored by the Students for a Democratic Society (SDS). All Americans were urged to participate "who agree with us that the war in Vietnam injures both Vietnamese and Americans, and should be stopped." The March brought 25,000 to the nation's capital to picket the White House, parade down the Mall to the Capitol where a statement was presented to Congress calling for an end to the war, and gather at a meeting addressed by student and adult speakers. Early in June, 17,500 students and adults packed Madison Square Garden in New York City to voice their concern over the Vietnam war. They applauded when a speaker declared: "We will not be quiet." They cheered when Senator Wayne Morse insisted that foreign policy belongs to the American people, not to the President, and when Mrs. Martin Luther King denounced the war as "immoral." Finally, they voiced agreement with Clark Kisinger of SDS that "our problem is in America, not in Vietnam. Through political action we must achieve the radical reconstruction of American foreign policy."[10]

In these and other public protest demonstrations of 1965, trade union members participated, many displaying buttons or wearing caps of their particular locals. But as yet no union had officially and publicly associated itself with the anti-war movement. The first to do so was Local 1199, Drug and Hospital Employees Union. On February 24, 1965, the union officials sent the following telegram to President Johnson and New York Senators Robert F. Kennedy and Jacob Javits:

We, the undersigned officers of the Executive Council, Local 1199, Drug and Hospital Employees Union, representing 25,000 members, urge an all-out effort to negotiate a peaceful settlement on Vietnam. We are unalterably opposed to extension of the war—a war no one can win. The present conflict can only be resolved by political not military means. We fervently seek your support to negotiate a peaceful settlement around the conference table.

The telegram was signed by Leon J. Davis, president; William J. Taylor, first vice president; Edward Ayash, treasurer; Moe Foner, executive secretary; five vice presidents and 16 members of the executive council.[11]

No other labor group took similar action until May 1965. At the fifth annual convention of the Negro American Labor Council,* May 28–30, the delegates unanimously adopted a "World Peace" resolution submitted by A. Philip Randolph, president of the NALC, which included an appeal that the war "be stopped in Vietnam and a negotiated peace be initiated" by the nations involved. "Military action is no remedy for the set-

---

* The Negro American Labor Council came into being as a protest against the abuses of racial discrimination within the labor movement. It was founded by A. Philip Randolph, and had as its purpose the "elimination of segregation and discrimination in labor, government and industry."

tlement of the problem in Southeast Asia or Santo Domingo,"* the resolution also declared. In addition to Randolph, others who urged the black unionists to adopt the resolution urging an end to the Vietnam war included Reverend Dr. Martin Luther King, president of the Southern Christian Leadership Conference; Bayard Rustin, executive director of the Randolph Institute; Cleveland Robinson, secretary-treasurer of District 65 of the Retail, Wholesale and Department Store Workers Union and national vice president of the NALC, and Gilberto Gerena-Valentin, president of the National Association for Puerto Rican Rights.[12]

The May 9, 1965 issue of *Missouri Teamster,* official journal of the St. Louis area Teamsters District Council headed by Harold Gibbons, carried an editorial critical of U.S. policy in the Dominican Republic and Vietnam. Although the editorial did not call for an end to the war in Vietnam, and while it declared that the union wished to see the triumph of "freedom" over communism, it insisted that the "containment of communism" policy was no longer valid. It described the Vietcong as a "native South Vietnamese force," and conceded that some had undoubtedly turned to communism, but went on to ask: "Where else can they turn?" It continued: "And our course of backing the reactionary supporters of the status quo, not only hardens Vietcong hostility to the U.S.—we become their best recruiters. And while we pursue this bland path, other patriots of southeast Asia become cynical at our talk about the freedom of men."

The August 1965 issue of *The 65er,* official journal of District 65, Retail, Wholesale and Department Store Workers Union, AFL-CIO, carried two items on the war in Vietnam. In an editorial, President David Livingston answered the question, "Vietnam: 'White Man's War'?" as follows:

Our war in Vietnam bids fair to unite the whole colored world against us. Our country may yet pay a terrible price for the wanton destruction we bring to Vietnam. The evi-

---

* The reference is to the military intervention in the Dominican Republic by the United States in April 1965.

dence suggests that the hatred in former colonial countries burns deep. . . . It's time to call a halt. If we continue as we are going, we might be winning the battle in Vietnam and losing our last chances to establish peace—not just with the Viet Cong nor North Vietnam nor in Southeast Asia, but with the whole colored world. . . . It is time for the ordinary people to be heard, to guide our country's leaders back to America's traditional belief in common decency—as a guide to action abroad as well as at home.

The 65er also carried the news that Assistant Vice President Al Evanoff, chairman of the District 65 Peace Action Committee, presented a statement on the war at a two-day unofficial Congressional hearings on Vietnam held in New York City on August 12–13 and called by Democratic Congressman William F. Ryan.* The statement read by Evanoff declared that "the immediate objective of American policy in Vietnam must be to stop the killing. The ultimate objective must be to allow the Vietnamese to determine for themselves who shall govern them, and what forms their government and their economies shall take." The statement called for an end to the "pointless" bombing of North Vietnam, an immediate cease-fire, and a return to the provisions of the Geneva Agreement of 1964. "The United States," it continued, "has neither a legal nor a moral right to be in Vietnam. Our presence is in contravention of international agreements; our commitment of troops and our participation in the Vietnamese civil war is unconstitutional." American policy in Vietnam, the statement concluded, "has led us to appear before the world as the white oppressor of non-white people."

These early small voices of opposition to U.S. policy in Vietnam were drowned out by the action of the AFL-CIO Executive Council applauding the Johnson Administration's extension of the war into North Vietnam. Indeed, Max Greenberg, President of RWDSU, in an editorial in the union's *Record* of November 14, 1965 urged the American people not to be fooled into thinking that the "small minority" in the labor move-

---

* Local 1199, Drug and Hospital Workers, was the only other labor union represented at the two-day hearings.

An appeal to our President
From 1,268 drug and hospital workers
Members, Local 1199, Drug and Hospital Employees Union,
RWDSU, AFL-CIO

NEGOTIATE— DON'T ESCALATE THE WAR IN VIETNAM

Every day precious American and Vietnamese lives are being lost in a war nobody can win; a war that can spark a world conflagration.

WE BELIEVE
There can be no military solution to this war.
This war must end at the conference table.
Our government should undertake new actions to speed that day.

WE ASK OUR GOVERNMENT TO

Stop the bombings

Seek an immediate cease-fire

Negotiate an international settlement

We ask our government to announce our willingness to include all parties directly involved, including the Vietcong, in any approach to a settlement; to reiterate our support for the withdrawal of all foreign military forces and the peaceful reunification of Vietnam with the right of the people to choose their own government.

Let us demonstrate that the U.S. is truly a leader in advancing the cause of peace and freedom and de-escalating war.

From an advertisement in the New York Times, *November 23, 1965, placed by 1,268 members of Local 1199, Drug and Hospital Employees Union.*

ment which opposed the Vietnam war represented any but a handful of "vocal" elements. Echoing the Johnson Administration, Greenberg argued that the "peace" voices in the labor movement were serving the cause of the enemies of the United States by "strengthening the Communists' resolve not to negotiate."

Local 1199, affiliated to the international union which Greenberg headed, was not intimidated by the implication that it was practically guilty of "treason" for opposing the war. The *New York Times* of November 23, 1965 carried an advertisement inserted by the Drug and Hospital Workers Ad Hoc Committee on Vietnam and paid for by voluntary contributions of $1 or more by 1,268 members of the union whose names appeared below their appeal to the President of the United States urging: "NEGOTIATE—DON'T ESCALATE THE WAR IN VIETNAM."

The advertisement went on to ask the government to (1) stop the bombings, (2) seek an immediate cease-fire, and (3) negotiate an international settlement. It urged the announcement of America's willingness to include the Vietcong in all negotiations; called for the withdrawal of all foreign military forces and the peace-ful reunification of Vietnam with the right of the people to choose their own government. It closed with the ap-peal: "Let us demonstrate that the U.S. is truly a leader in advancing the cause of peace and freedom and de-es-calating war." On November 27 members of 1199 were among 30,000 at an anti-war demonstration in Wash-ington.

Many readers of the *New York Times* were undoubt-edly surprised to see trade unionists publicly voice senti-ments which, in the eyes of the labor establishment, were tantamount to "giving aid and comfort to the enemy." But others had probably come to expect such a bold departure from the usual trade union approach to social issues from members of Local 1199. Already the Drug and Hospital Employees Union had gained the reputation of doing the unexpected and unusual in the labor movement. While it had played a leading role, along with other unions, in support of the civil rights movement in the South, making its presence felt at Birmingham, Selma, Montgomery and other protest demonstrations, it had gone beyond the vast majority of trade unions by organizing and improving the working conditions of thousands of underpaid and overworked black and Puerto Rican hospital workers. Not content merely to unionize the hitherto neglected hospital workers, the union leadership had involved them in a wide range of educational and cultural activities which had brought the political level of the union's membership to a point where they understood earlier and more clearly than most workers that more guns meant less butter and that the Johnson Administration's "war on poverty" was already being emasculated by the mounting costs of the war in Vietnam.

One other aspect of Local 1199 made it something of a maverick in organized labor. When its membership took a position on social issues, its leadership did not ignore their views and contradict them in their own statements and actions. This was not true in the case of the United Auto Workers. In 1965 that union had gone on record against escalation of the war and had called for serious steps for peace. But shortly thereafter Reuther and a majority of the executive board proceeded strongly to endorse President Johnson's policy of escalation. Reuther even joined Richard Nixon and other advocates of war escalation in endorsing a Freedom House statement supporting the Johnson Administration's conduct of the war and accusing anti-war dissenters of impeding a peaceful solution by encouraging North Vietnam's "illusion" that the American people favored their cause.[13]

How far in advance Local 1199 was in 1965 of the main body of organized labor was illustrated by the shameful events that transpired in December at the AFL-CIO convention in San Francisco. The 928 delegates had barely gathered when the Executive Council proposed, as the first order of business, endorsement of its recommendation to raise George Meany's salary from $45,000 to $70,000. The first two days of the convention were devoted largely to mobilizing the AFL-

CIO fully behind the Johnson Administration's foreign policy. President Johnson, via telephone, Vice President Humphrey, Secretary of State Rusk, Undersecretary Alexis Johnson, and the national commander of the American Legion followed each other with speeches lauding the conduct of the war in Vietnam. Then Meany delivered no fewer than four speeches endorsing the Administration's handling of the war.

The Convention adopted, without discussion or dissent, a policy statement hailing U.S. military intervention in the Dominican Republic. President Johnson was applauded for having sent 20,000 troops to the Caribbean island and thus preventing "another Cuban-type regime." The Convention then turned to Vietnam. But even before it had dealt with this issue, a slight reflection of the existing opposition in some parts of the labor movement to the war found expression during the discussion on the economic policy resolution. A. Philip Randolph touched on the war when he warned of the already evident effort to use the operations in Vietnam as an excuse to foist the burden of its cost upon the backs of the poor and sidetrack the advance of civil rights. Cleveland Robinson, black delegate of the Retail, Wholesale and Department Store Union, secretary-treasurer of District 65 and vice president of the Negro American Labor Council, carried Randolph's point further. Pointing to the contradiction between Vietnam and the prospects for a "Great Society," Robinson said:

I join with Brother Randolph in my fears that this present conflict, now raging in Vietnam will be used as the excuse to curtail even the little we are now getting. I do raise questions about the wisdom of what we are doing. I do not pretend that we have all the answers, but I will say this. Brother chairman and delegates, our history has been replete with those who have found it necessary amidst the din of popularity to cast a voice of dissent because they feel it right in their conscience to dissent. Were it not for the dissent of such people our government would not be where it stands today. . . .

So let us not be cocksure of what's right and what's wrong. Let's make sure that we all listen to each other, exchange our ideas as true patriots.[14]

But there was no room for dissent on Vietnam, and no delegate had the courage during the debate on the issue to voice opposition to the barrage of pro-Administration propaganda which deluged the convention. Students from the University of California at Berkeley and San Francisco State College, seated in the balcony listened with mounting anger, disgust, and frustration to the parade of Administration apologists for escalation and the endorsement of their views by Meany. Unable to take it any longer, they began to voice their dissent in shouts from the balcony. The *New York Times* described what followed:

The protesters shouted such things as "Get out of Vietnam!" and "Labor fakers!" and then began to chant, "Debate! Debate! Debate!"

The union delegates raised a chorus of booing and cries of "Get out of here!" "Get a haircut!" and "Go to Russia and debate!"

George Meany, AFL-CIO president, pounded the lectern with his gavel and boomed: "Will the sergeant of arms clear these kookies out of the gallery."[15]

Not a single delegate arose to rebuke Meany and uphold the right of dissent, although late in the convention Emil Mazey of the United Auto Workers did remind the assembled unionists that labor had fought hard for the right to disagree and should defend the right for others. He went on to deplore Meany's disdain for and harsh treatment of the Vietnam protesters. The *New York Times* reported that his speech received "scant applause."[16]

The original draft of the Vietnam resolution had been modified before it was presented to the delegates, at Reuther's request, to include a nod in the direction of negotiations. This gesture toward a peaceful solution of the war had been opposed by Meany, but, according to reporters, it was inserted "after Vice President Humphrey indicated to the union leaders . . . that the Johnson Administration would not like to see a divisive controversy erupt on the floor."[17] The Administration had no reason to be anything but pleased with the compromise resolution since it placed the AFL-CIO behind its Vietnam policy, and included a labor version of the Senate's Tonkin Resolution by endorsing in advance "all measures the Administration might deem necessary to halt Communist aggression and secure a just and lasting peace."

In the floor discussion preceding the unanimous adoption of the resolution, Meany and Reuther explained their understanding of its meaning. The difference between them, if it existed at all, has been properly characterized as "very hazy." Both rejected U.S. withdrawal from Vietnam; both wanted it made clear to Hanoi and Peking that they would not gain a military victory, and both endorsed the principle of finding a solution at the conference table. Reuther, however, insisted that his views stood at "midpoint between two extreme positions"—the advocates of "unlimited escalation," on the one hand, and that of the "appeasers" on the other.[18] Whether he realized it or not, by labeling as "appeasers" the advocates of a negotiated settlement as the only way to achieve peace, he was lending fuel to the arguments of the AFL-CIO "hawks."

The Vietnam resolution, adopted unanimously, was a clear signal to the Johnson Administration that it could continue escalating the war without being concerned about organized labor's reaction. Undoubtedly, there were delegates who were disturbed by the lengths to which the hierarchy had gone to line the organization behind the Administration's Vietnam policy. "Some liberal union leaders said they thought it unwise," wrote the reporter for the *New York Times,* "to give President Johnson a blank check in the war, and they expressed dismay about it privately."[19] Since their doubts were never voiced on the floor, the sixth constitutional convention of the AFL-CIO conveyed to the world the message that the main body of organized labor in America promised in advance, without a dissenting vote, to support any Administration action in the war.

How much this vote represented the thinking of the AFL-CIO membership is difficult to determine accurately. But before one can conclude that it reflected the point of view of the millions of members of the AFL-

CIO, it would be well to understand that by far the greatest number of votes at this and all other conventions of the organization—some estimate it at 95 percent of the vote[20]—come from appointed, not elected, delegates. Nearly all delegates are chosen by the general executive board of their respective unions. Since unions cast as many votes as their per-capita payments, as few as ten of the largest unions can cast as many votes as the rest of the convention; as few as 15 of the former AFL unions could outvote the rest of the convention.

The fact that at the 1965 AFL-CIO convention some of the delegates did express their concern over the stand taken on Vietnam, even though privately, was not without significance. This reflected a growing uneasiness in some sections of organized labor at the increasing isolation of the labor movement from socially-minded Americans. To Meany and his colleagues, as probably to the vast majority of the delegates, the youthful dissenters in the balcony were "kookies," but to those who voiced their dismay to the *New York Times* reporter, the cries from the balcony symbolized the fact that the youth of America, and not labor as in the thirties, was a leading spokesman for the dispossessed. Young Americans now saw organized labor as the voice of the Establishment. These delegates knew, too, that unless there were those in labor's ranks who spoke with a different voice, large sections of the American people, along with the dedicated youngsters in the colleges and universities, would be lost to the labor movement as allies. Already it was becoming difficult, if not impossible, to halt their complete alienation from organized labor. The day would certainly come when the trade unions, as in the thirties, would need allies, and it would not be simple, if present policies persisted, to overcome the years of indifference, indeed, of hostility, to those who should be organized labor's allies.

Events in 1966 strengthened the feeling of dismay at the course the AFL-CIO was pursuing and revealed the existence of a serious rift in the top leadership of the organization as a result of these policies. It was Walter Reuther who led the battle that developed over foreign

We Take Our Stand for Peace and an End to the War in Vietnam

ALLIANCE FOR LABOR ACTION

International Union, UAW
Walter P. Reuther, President
Emil Mazey, Secretary Treasurer

International Brotherhood of Teamsters
Frank E. Fitzsimmons, General Vice President
Thomas E. Flynn, General Secretary Treasurer

International Chemical Workers Union
Thomas E. Boyle, President
Marshall Shafer, Secretary Treasurer

An invitation to the

FOUNDING CONFERENCE TRADE UNION DIVISION of SANE

Tuesday, May 3 at 2 pm
METHODIST OFFICE for the UN
777 UN PLAZA NYC

This invitation to form the Trade Union Division of SANE in 1966 was sponsored by top officials of 17 local unions in the New York area.

The Alliance for Labor Action, formed in June 1969, urged an immediate end to the war in Vietnam.

policy. Reuther publicly objected when AFL-C
gates to a European labor conference walked
cause delegates from Communist-bloc countr
seated. Meany defended and supported the actio
was followed by the revelations of the connectio
tween the AFL-CIO's International Affairs Depa
and the Central Intelligence Agency. The frequen
gations in magazines and newspapers as far ba
1962 of cooperation between the AFL-CIO lea
ship, particularly Meany and Lovestone, and the
had been dismissed by most trade union leaders
"muckraking by outsiders." But when in May 1966,
the course of the UAW convention in Los Angeles, V
tor Reuther publicly stated that the AFL-CIO's Intern
tional Affairs Department was involved with the CIA
and went on to denounce the influence exerted by Love
stone as having been responsible for "the tragedy o
AFL-CIO activities in foreign affairs," the issue could
no longer be brushed aside.

As additional evidence of the AFL-CIO-CIA connections kept piling up, the impact of the revelations increased. The ranks of those in the unions who had been
privately voicing their doubts over the direction of the
AFL-CIO's foreign policy positions increased, and a
number of them were now even prepared to voice their
differences publicly. Thus the United Automobile
Workers, after calling attention to its record of "contin-
uous and successful struggle against communism and all
other forms of totalitarianism," characterized the foreign
policy approach of the Meany leadership as rigid and
inflexible, and charged that, in general, Meany's leadership "suffers from a sense of complacency and adher-
ence to the status quo and is not fulfilling the basic aims
and purposes which prompted the merger of the AFL-
CIO." While some critics held that Reuther's differences with Meany stemmed from the latter's unwillingness to retire and allow the UAW president to fill the
top office of the AFL-CIO, and others questioned how
consistently he would adhere to a position differing
from that of Meany's or how actively he would oppose
the latter's stand on foreign policy, it was clear to many

that the Reuther-Meany conflict over foreign policy would have an important bearing on labor's position on the war in Vietnam.

On March 26, 1966, New York City's demonstration against the Vietnam war saw more than 50,000 march in protest, including a contingent which walked behind a banner reading, "Trade Unionists for Peace." Among the trade unionists in the line of march were a number who were becoming increasingly disturbed by the AFL-CIO high command's unswerving, uncritical allegiance to the Administration's course in Vietnam. Following the demonstration, they met and decided to organize the Trade Union Division of SANE (National Committee for Sane Nuclear Policy).* Late in April, these trade unionists issued a leaflet announcing the Founding Conference, May 3, at the Methodist Office for the UN. It read:

The war in Viet Nam affects all Americans and deeply concerns millions. Many have spoken out in the growing debate to which the Fulbright Committee of the Senate made so great a contribution. But one group of Americans conspicuous by their absence from the national dialogue has been organized labor. We intend to rectify this condition.

In the brief few days following an initial conference, there has been an outpouring of support for the proposal to form a Trade Union Division of SANE. It is clear now that many trade union leaders have been waiting for just such a suggestion.

You are invited to participate in this historic occasion.

The historic invitation for the historic occasion was sponsored by:

Rudolph Abt, president, Local 101, Transport Workers Union; Leon J. Davis, president, Local 1199; Frank Dutto, president, Local 3, Bakery and Confectionery Workers; Thomas Flavell, manager, Local 169, Amalgamated Clothing Workers; Henry Foner, president, Joint Board, Fur, Leather and Machine Workers Union; Victor Gotbaum,

---

* SANE was founded in 1957 to work for a nuclear test-ban treaty. Its official title was changed in 1969 to SANE—Citizens' Organization for a Sane World.

director, District 37, State, County, Municipal Workers of America; Edward Gray, assistant director, United Auto Workers, Region 9; John Hoh, president, Brewery Workers Union, Local 3; Joel R. Jacobson, president, New Jersey State Industrial Union Council; David Livingston, president, District 65; Richard McManus, president, Local 8–149, Oil, Chemical and Atomic Workers; James McNamara, manager, Local 102, United Hatters, Cap and Millinery Workers; Sam Meyers, president, Local 259, United Auto Workers; Albert Shanker, president, Local 2, United Federation of Teachers; Alex Sirota, president, Local 140, United Furniture Workers; Arduilo Susi, president, Local 89, Chefs, Cooks, Pastry Cooks and Assistants Union, and Leon Sverdlove, president, Local 1, Jewelry Workers Union.

As James A. Wechsler pointed out in the New York *Post* of May 4, 1966 the men associated with this call "belong to the second and third echelons of the labor movement; few are headline figures." But he also noted that their action reflected "growing restiveness in many labor sectors over the monolithic militancy (or meekness) that has characterized the AFL-CIO role in a great national debate," and the fact that though these men were "not celebrated luminaries of labor," they had "stepped forward in a certain defiance of labor's Establishment is symptomatic of a frustration and unrest that many observers detected beneath the surface of the last AFL-CIO convention."

A policy statement was adopted unanimously by the 173 union officers and staff members present at the founding conference, representing 30 local unions in the Metropolitan area. Pointing out that no American was unaffected by the war, that more and more Americans were speaking out on the issue of Vietnam, the statement declared:

It becomes increasingly clear that the simple solution to the Viet Nam war offered again and again—"victory through escalation"—cannot succeed. It is clear also that negotiations must take place among all those involved in the armed struggle. We urge steps to bring about such negotiations, rather than further escalation of the conflict. . . .

It is incumbent on Americans in all walks of life to come to understand, through discussion and debate, the issues which this unhappy war raises for our future relationships with the people of Viet Nam, of Asia and of the undeveloped countries all over the globe.

Trade unionists have a special responsibility to contribute to this discussion. Our aspirations to help build a great society at home in a peaceful world, are placed in jeopardy by the increasing tempo of American involvement in the war. . . .

The initial policy statement, it is clear, was not directed against the AFL-CIO leadership and did not spell out any specific course of action for the nation to follow in ending the war. Basically, the policy statement was a plea for free discussion within labor's ranks, and an end to a course of action consisting of regular statements of labor's allegiance to the President's escalation of the war.

Following the founding conference, union leaders from 12 states met in Washington for an exchange of views on extending the Trade Union Division to other areas. By June 1966 preliminary meetings had been held in Chicago and San Francisco to establish similar groups, and discussions were already under way among union leaders for the same purpose in St. Louis, Detroit, Cleveland, Boston, Philadelphia, Los Angeles and the Southwest.

At the same time, at four union conventions, all held during the week of May 23, the existence of a new and questioning attitude toward the war became apparent. While the emphasis varied, each of the four unions warned against escalation of the war. The sharpest stand was taken by the United Packinghouse Workers Union in a resolution submitted by its International Executive Board and strongly endorsed by President Ralph Helstein who spoke firmly against the bombing of cities and civilians and the mining of harbors. The Packinghouse resolution, adopted after full floor debate, declared: "The basic and urgent objective of our national policy should be to end the war in Vietnam." It called upon the United States to "deal in good faith with any and all nations and groups . . . and proclaim our willingness to halt all bombings and join in an immediate 'cease fire.' " The union also hailed the discussion and debate on the war as "a sign of strength, not weakness, for a democratic nation . . . willing and able to reexamine its policies through open debate and discussion among its citizens and leaders." It condemned "the unthinking and irresponsible demands that we bomb cities and civilians, and mine harbors even at the risk of open conflict with other nations."

Meeting the same week, the United Auto Workers took a much weaker stand. It rejected a unilateral pullout and escalation as "unacceptable alternatives," urged more strenuous efforts to negotiate a peaceful end to the war, and called for the recognition of China and its admission into the United Nations. Since the resolution did not come to the convention floor until the end of the sessions, on Saturday morning when over half the delegates had left for home, there was little discussion on the issue. However, UAW Secretary-Treasurer Emil Mazey called for a national conference of UAW members on the issue, plus regional conferences to place the union more solidly behind the peace movement. He also defended the right of some two dozen young peace demonstrators who had waved anti-intervention placards when President Johnson addressed the convention by phone.

The Retail, Wholesale and Department Store Union expressed the belief at its convention that there is a "growing concern" among the American people "as to whether the course we are now following in Viet Nam is the correct one." The convention rejected both a pullout and escalation as solutions, calling for negotiations as "the only way."

However, at the Amalgamated Clothing Workers convention, the issue of Vietnam dominated the speeches and the meeting. Secretary-General U Thant of the UN, in his address to the delegates, urged a scaling down of American military operations in Vietnam, the utilization of the UN in peace endeavors, and called for direct negotiations with all powers concerned, including

China and the National Liberation Front. He received a standing ovation. The convention also cheered Secretary-Treasurer Frank Rosenblum, one of the most outspoken critics of Vietnam policy in the labor movement, as he lashed out at U.S. involvement in the war, charging that the war was immoral and could lead to total destruction of mankind. He cried: "We are supposed to be fighting for freedom, but the question is: freedom from whom? We are not wanted there and we cannot possibly win the war in Vietnam." Rosenblum went far beyond most union critics of the war by proposing that the United States withdraw from Vietnam. The convention did not go this far. Its resolution rejected the policy of escalation and called for persistent negotiations until peace was achieved. It urged worldwide disarmament to "free the billions of dollars now spent for arms which should be spent for food and shelter and books and hospitals . . . abundance will be only a dream while all nations spend half or more of their national income on the weapons of war." Like the Packinghouse Workers, the Clothing Workers hailed the critics of Vietnam policy and called for debate and discussion.

The resolutions of these conventions were published in the first issue of Trade Union Division *Sane World* of June 1966 under the headline, "Unionists Speak Out on Vietnam War—At Last!" The four-page issue also included a statement by U Thant, which declared: "The labor movement, with its vast influence and prestige, can be a very powerful force in producing the changes of attitude which will be required. The task is great and the time is certainly short. The choice may well be between ruin and the fulfillment of all we have dreamt of."

U Thant had made this comment in an address to the Amalgamated Clothing Workers Convention. On June 20 he announced a three-point program for ending the war in Vietnam: (1) cessation of bombing of North Vietnam, (2) scaling down of all military activities in South Vietnam, leading to an effective cease-fire, and (3) willingness of all sides to enter into discussions with all those who are actually doing the fighting, including the National Liberation Front. The Trade Union Divi-

sion of SANE promptly came out in support of U
Thant's three-point program for ending a war which the
UN Secretary-General had called "one of the most bar-
barous" in history. Members of unions affiliated to the
Division made the rounds of factories, shops and public
centers soliciting signatures to a petition issued by the
organization. The petition was topped by quotations
from U Thant warning that if the war in Vietnam continued it would lead to World War III and urging the
"cessation of the bombing of North Vietnam." This was
followed by:

Trade Unionists Say:
Negotiation NOW in Vietnam!
We trade unionists are confronted almost daily with the
choice of one of two courses of action: either constant,
senseless strife—or negotiations. . . .
We in organized labor have chosen the only way out of
conflicts that makes sense—that of negotiation. We urge
the same course upon our country and its leaders.[21]

The activities of the Trade Union Division of SANE
were not entirely ignored by the AFL-CIO Executive
Council. Meeting in Chicago in August 1966, with Walter Reuther absent, the Council unanimously adopted a
statement on Vietnam that was even more hawkish than
the San Francisco resolution. It once again wholeheart-
edly supported Johnson's policies, endorsing the buildup
of American troops. But, after a hypocritical gesture toward the right of minority dissent, it condemned all opponents of the war in the United States. The statement
read in part: "Those who would deny our military
forces unstinting support are, in effect, aiding the Communist enemy of our country—at the very moment
when it is bearing the heaviest burdens in the defense of
world peace and freedom."

Reuther later called the statement "intemperate, hys-
terical, jingoistic, and unworthy of a policy statement of
a free labor movement." On November 14 a review of
all AFL-CIO foreign policy positions, requested by
Reuther earlier in the year, was held. In Reuther's absence—he gave as an excuse the necessity of having to
attend his own union's executive board meeting—the

Executive Council, to no one's surprise, reaffirmed the 19 different positions on American foreign policy it had taken in the previous 11 years. All were reaffirmed unanimously except for the Council's long-standing opposition to U.S. recognition of Communist China. On this issue, Jacob Potofsky of the Amalgamated cast the only dissenting vote.[22]

Reuther's absence from the Executive Council's review of foreign policy has been criticized as indicating an unwillingness on his part "to wage a fight on the foreign policy issue when the time was most opportune."[23] Yet the breakaway of Reuther's group from the Meany-Lovestone forces, its exposure of the AFL-CIO's relations with the CIA, and Reuther's characterization of the Executive Council statement on Vietnam as "unworthy" of the labor movement had the effect of strengthening the rumblings of discontent in the trade unions over labor's foreign policy and helped bring into the open the demand for a change in that policy. On November 17, 1966, three days after the Executive Council had informed the world that, like the Bourbons, it had forgotten nothing and learned nothing, what proved to be a major break with official AFL-CIO policy occurred. On that day 250 union leaders in New York and New Jersey adopted a resolution roundly criticizing the AFL-CIO Executive Council for its support of Administration policy in Vietnam and calling for an immediate de-escalation of the war. The statement was issued under the name of the Trade Union Division of SANE.

The *New York Times* of November 18, 1966 which reported the action under the heading, "Unionists Score AFL-CIO on War," noted that the unionists at the meeting, officers or staff members of a cross-section of 31 unions, "have been associated in the past with political causes of both the left and the right," but had joined together in criticizing "the national leadership of the AFL-CIO . . . for supporting the Johnson Administration policies in Vietnam and called for an immediate de-escalation of the war." The resolution, the report continued, had been read by Joel R. Jacobson, president of the New Jersey State Industrial Council, and among those who spoke for its adoption were Edward Gray, assistant director of Region 9 of the United Automobile Workers.

Mr. Gray noted . . . that the resolution was "as far as we can go right now." He and other speakers noted that they did not pretend to represent the views of a majority of the union movement, but that they did express the views of a minority. This minority, they said, should be heard because, as the resolution stated, "the war has already cost too much," and "the moral integrity and reputation of the nation has been compromised."

The resolution had been drawn up by a committee composed, among others, of Leon J. Davis, president of Local 1199 at whose headquarters the meeting was held; John Hoh, president, Local 3 of the Brewery Workers Union; Victor Gotbaum, director, District Council 37, American Federation of State, County and Municipal Employees Union, and August Bellanca, international vice president of the Amalgamated Clothing Workers. It was the most advanced statement on the war thus far issued by the Trade Union Division of SANE and the first in which the organization publicly broke with the AFL-CIO leadership:

The existence and activities of the Trade Union Division of SANE testifies to the fact that another position on the war commands the support of many responsible trade union officials. We are encouraged to see our ranks growing, and the formation of affiliated groups in other cities. We intend to go forward along these lines with as much energy as we can muster. In so doing, we reject the allegation made at an earlier AFL-CIO Executive Council meeting that "while a minority has the right to dissent from the majority, disruption by even a well-meaning minority can only pollute and poison the bloodstream of our democracy." On the contrary, our activities are dedicated to the finest democratic traditions of the labor movement—the traditions of free discussion and debate.[24]

On February 8, 1967, Walter Reuther issued his new "Program for the American Labor Movement." It proposed that organized labor again become the champion of social reforms benefiting all members of society, and

that the labor unions should once again occupy the forefront position in the struggle for racial equality, civil lib-
erties, educational reform, aid to elderly citizens, the
conservation of natural resources, and the war against
poverty. On foreign policy it reiterated Reuther's anti-
communism, but favored "building bridges of international understanding leading toward a reduction of armaments and the building of a just and enduring peace
in which people with diverse economic and social sys-
tems might live peacefully."

Although the "Program for the American Labor
Movement" said nothing about the war in Vietnam, its
appearance strengthened the labor groups beginning to
voice opposition to the Meany-AFL-CIO Executive
Council's uncritical endorsement of the war. By the
spring of 1967 chapters of the Trade Union Division of
SANE had been formed in the Midwest and the Far
West. An event which attracted nationwide publicity
was the formation in December 1966 of the Chicago
chapter of the Trade Union Division of SANE. The
sponsorship included a cross-section of the labor movement of the Chicago area, and the day-long conference
attracted 400 unionists. The featured speakers included
Frank Rosenblum, secretary-treasurer of the Clothing
Workers and Ralph Helstein, president of the Packinghouse Workers. Rosenblum denounced the role of the
United States in Vietnam, which he called "interfering
in what is essentially a civil war . . . against world
opinion . . . in the name of freedom and humane
ideals. . . . In the name of freedom we are conducting
one of the most brutal wars in history, taking few prisoners."

Among labor leaders who participated in the conference and a series of panel discussions were Robert Gib-
son, secretary-treasurer of the Illinois AFL-CIO State
Federation of Labor; Abe Feinglass, vice president of
the Amalgamated Meat Cutters; Timuel L. Black, president of the Negro American Labor Council, and
Charles Hayes, director of Packinghouse Workers District 1. Packinghouse President Ralph Helstein evalu-
ated the conference as an important reassertion of la-

bor's historic role in the search for a peaceful world. He urged the linking of the civil rights, labor and peace movements, and that the first item on all future agendas be ending the war in Vietnam. Following the conference, Murray Finley of the Clothing Workers, the gathering's chairman, told the press: "Meany and Johnson do not reflect the thinking of the American people. Never before in American history has there been so little enthusiasm for fighting a war."[25]

On March 21, 1967, the Chicago *Sun* carried a full-page advertisement announcing a Peace Parade and Public Rally to End the War in Vietnam to be held four days later. Among the ten sponsors was the Chicago Trade Union Division of SANE. (Others included the Midwest Faculty Committee on Vietnam, Veterans for Peace in Vietnam, and the Chicago Fellowship of Reconciliation.) Five speakers were to address the rally, among them: Dr. Martin Luther King, Jr.; Dr. Benjamin Spock, co-chairman of National SANE; and Emil Mazey, secretary-treasurer of the United Auto Workers. Readers of the *Sun* were urged to join the sponsors of the demonstration in calling upon the government to: end the bombing of North and South Vietnam, initiate an immediate cease-fire, agree to negotiate directly with all parties to the dispute, including the national liberation front, and make a clear commitment to withdraw our troops from Vietnam on the principle of self-determination for the Vietnamese people.

The March 25th anti-war demonstration was significant in two ways: It marked the first time Martin Luther King had led a peace march. ("We must combine the fervor of the civil rights movement with the peace movement," he told the demonstrators.) It also marked the first time a trade union division of SANE had publicly united with other groups in a peace demonstration. A number of top leaders of the trade unions, who probably shared the misgivings about the war voiced by those of their organizations who had associated themselves with the Trade Union Division, had stayed aloof so that they might be in the position to repudiate their lieutenants if the pressure to end the war relaxed. Nevertheless, this was the first open break of a significant group of AFL-CIO leaders with the Meany-Lovestone policies, a repudiation of the cold war approach which had dominated the labor movement for two decades.

On one point there could be no doubt. The battle to associate the labor movement with the forces seeking to end the war in Vietnam had begun.

**LOCAL 590,
DISTRICT COUNCIL 33, AFSCME
has sent the following telegram to
George Meany, President of the
AFL-CIO:**

In protest against President Nixon's actions to continue and expand the war in Southeast Asia, actions which clearly are in excess of his legal presidential powers, we, the members of local 590, American Federation of State, County and Municipal Employees, district council 33, urge you to call a nationwide general strike of all AFL-CIO members.

From an advertisement in the Philadelphia Daily News, *May 8, 1970.*

3

LABOR ASSEMBLY FOR PEACE

IN MID-MAY 1967 A "SUPPORT THE BOYS" MARCH DOWN NEW YORK'S FIFTH AVENUE FEATURED LARGE AND vocal contingents from the National Maritime Union with "My country right or wrong" signs, and equally vocal groups from the International Longshoremen's Association, the Teamsters Joint Council, Motion Picture Operators, Engineers, Composition Roofers and Water Proofers, Bricklayers No. 34, Tile Layer Helpers and others. Some carried signs demanding "Bomb Moscow," "Bomb Peking," "Drop the H Bomb on Hanoi." Now and then members of these union contingents would join John Birchers, Minutemen, and American Legionaires and together jump from the march to beat up any bystander who expressed support for peace.[1]

About the time these unionists were displaying their support for the war, with a touch of brutality added, a conference was being held in Chicago of leaders of the Trade Union Division of SANE chapters in New York, Los Angeles and Chicago, along with Amalgamated Clothing Workers directors in the mid-west and southwest, as well as trade union leaders from Pittsburgh, Washington, Minneapolis, St. Paul, Cleveland, Milwaukee, Detroit, St. Louis and San Francisco. All told, there were about 40 union leaders present, including Frank Rosenblum of the Amalgamated Clothing Workers, Pat Gorman of the Amalgamated Meat Cutters, and Victor Reuther's staff man, Stanley Greenspan.

The conference agreed to set up chapters of the Trade Union Division of SANE in new cities; issue new and more materials on why labor should support an immediate negotiated settlement of the war, and to call a national labor leadership conference on the war in

Chicago in the fall of 1967. Early in the fall a call went out for the Conference to be held at the Center for Continuing Education, University of Chicago, November 11–12, Veterans' Day weekend. The Call issued under the auspices of the Trade Union Division of SANE featured the fact that Frank Rosenblum, Patrick E. Gorman, Al Hartung, retired president of the International Woodworkers of America, and Emil Mazey invited trade union leaders to participate in a "National Labor Leadership Assembly for Peace." They noted:

The annual cost of the war to America will soon reach 30 billion dollars a year. This enormous diversion of human wealth and energies into war has grievously undermined every program to meet the needs of our cities and has intensified the undercurrents of violence in our own land.

Young men who deserve better are dying in a war whose purpose they do not understand. The culture of our country is being brutalized by a logic which seeks to justify the use of the most inhumane weapons of war whose primary victims inevitably are the population of Vietnam—both North and South.

The Assembly would examine the impact of American foreign policy on the lives of the working class and "what other paths exist for us to achieve legitimate American objectives in the world today." Invited were "all trade union leaders, of whatever persuasion, to join with us in these deliberations at this most crucial hour in our nation's history."[2]

At the time this call was issued some 480,000 Americans were fighting in Vietnam. The cost of the war, as the call noted, was running at an annual rate close to $30 billion. The number of Americans killed in action, which had totaled 6,500 for the six-year period through 1966, was nearing the 9,000 mark (plus 60,000 wounded) for 1967 alone.

The organizers of the Labor Leadership Assembly for Peace expected about 250 to respond to their call. But 523 trade unionists from 38 states and 63 international unions, including 45 national officers, showed up in Chicago, most of whom paid their own way. For two days a wide range of speakers in and out of the labor movement—Norman Thomas, Martin Luther King, John K. Galbraith, Frank Rosenblum, Victor Reuther, Emil Mazey, David Schoenbrun, Rear Admiral Arnold L. True, Senators Vance Hartke and Eugene McCarthy, Seymour Melman of Columbia University, Robert F. Browne of Fairleigh Dickinson, and Russell Allen of Michigan State—addressed the Assembly. Some, like Norman Thomas, the veteran Socialist leader, appealed for immediate withdrawal of American troops from Vietnam and an immediate and unconditional cessation of bombing; others limited themselves to calling for an end to the bombing of North Vietnam, a cease-fire, and the immediate beginning of negotiations. But all speakers agreed that to succeed a peace movement had to have the support of labor and hailed the Assembly as an important initial step in this direction.

Opening the gathering, Rosenblum expressed regret that "the chief spokesman of American labor not only endorses the Administration's policies, but is if anything to the right of the Administration." Rosenblum then declared: "We must prove that he does not represent the largest segment of the labor movement. On the crucial question of peace, labor must be in the vanguard. We should be leaders, not followers." Mazey, a long-time opponent of the war in Vietnam and one of the few labor leaders who had protested Meany's callous handling of the peace demonstrators at the AFL-CIO convention in 1965, hit hard at those who would intimidate dissenters in the name of patriotism, declaring: "I believe that the greatest patriots of our country are those who have the courage to speak out when they think the President's actions are wrong. It is not the cry for an honorable peace that endangers our body, but the steady escalation of the war." Gorman, unable to attend because of his wife's illness, sent a message urging, "In the name of God, let's bring our boys back home with an established peace so that we need not hang our heads in shame, and this can best be accomplished at the conference table instead of on ghastly looking battlefields 8,000 miles away." Victor Reuther, director of the

UAW's International Affairs Department, not only called for an immediate cessation of the bombing of North Vietnam and the opening of negotiations for an end to the war with both the Hanoi government and the NLF, but reviewed the history of the Meany-Lovestone foreign policy activities abroad, and pointed out that they and their ilk had not only worked with the CIA but also with supporters of the John Birch Society and other right-wing, anti-union groups in the United States. Reuther concluded by calling for an end to the long-established practice in the American labor movement and especially of the AFL-CIO national leadership of devising and executing foreign policy without consulting or involving the workers:

The determination of foreign policy within the labor movement must not be permitted to remain the vest pocket operation of any individual or small leadership group. As with union collective bargaining objectives and domestic legislative goals, foreign policy decisions should flow upward from the membership following the widest possible discussion in depth by the rank and file.

Following the pattern set by the academic teach-ins, the Assembly broke up into work groups to discuss such issues as U.S. policy in Southeast Asia, China, nuclear arms, the American economy and the war, labor and the war, and social problems and the War. B. J. Widick, who covered the Assembly for *The Nation,* observed that the teach-ins at leading universities "would have difficulty improving on the intellectual content of these sessions."

After considerable discussion, during which some delegates criticized it as too moderate, the policy statement of the Labor Leadership Assembly for Peace was adopted. It urged: "American labor must play its part in bringing this savage war to a swift and just conclusion, so that we may devote our wealth and energies to the struggle against poverty, disease, hunger and bigotry."[3]

One should not exaggerate the significance of the Labor Leadership Assembly for Peace. After all, only four national leaders of the AFL-CIO—Gorman, Mazey, Rosenblum, and Hartung—would agree to sign the call for the gathering. Nevertheless, the weekend of

November 11–12, 1967 marked a milestone both in the history of the American labor movement and of the peace movement. While there had been a voice raised here and there in organized labor against the AFL-CIO's hard-line, cold-war foreign policy in general and its support of the Vietnamese war in particular, the Assembly marks a significant break with these policies.

To be sure, independent unions like the United Electrical, Radio, and Machine Workers, the International Longshoremen's and Warehousemen's Union on the West Coast, the International Fur and Leather Workers (now merged with the Amalgamated Meat Cutters), and the Mine, Mill and Smelter Workers (now merged with Steel), had long and consistently spoken out for a peaceful foreign policy. To be sure, too, Local 1199 and its president Leon Davis, District 65 of the Retail Workers and its head, David Livingston, and the Joint Board Fur, Leather and Machine Workers, headed by Henry Foner, had publicly opposed the Vietnam war from the beginning. But little attention had been paid to their voices, and the impression had long prevailed that in foreign policy the labor movement spoke with one voice —that of George Meany.

The Labor Leadership Assembly for Peace destroyed the impression of a monolithic labor structure in support of the war in Indochina. While the delegates represented only a minority of the trade union movement, the Assembly, nevertheless, was the first time that trade union leaders from all over the country had come together to challenge the AFL-CIO policy of unquestioning support for the war in Vietnam. Moreover, in expressing its opposition to the U.S. war policy in Vietnam, it brought a section of the American labor movement in line with organized labor the world over.

The second significance of the Chicago Labor Assembly is that it marked an important change in the character of the peace movement. Until November 1967, the opposition to the war in Vietnam had been conducted almost exclusively by academic, youth, church and professional groups with labor, on the whole, conspicuous by its absence. Now at long last an important, even though not the major, section of the labor movement had officially aligned itself with the peace movement.

There was a third significance of the Assembly, and this was pointed out most clearly by Charles P. Larrowe, Professor of Economics, Michigan State University, in a letter to *The Nation* of December 25, 1967. He wrote in part:

> For many of us an encouraging aspect of the National Labor Leadership Assembly for Peace was that it seemed a long step toward ending two decades of redbaiting in the labor movement. Sitting side by side with men and women from AFL-CIO unions in the discussions, indeed even appearing as panelists, were men from unions that have been in Coventry for eighteen years—since 1949, when the CIO expelled them on charges of "following the Communist Party line": the UE, the West Coast longshoremen, even the old United Public Workers, which sent a delegate from their 7,000-member local in Hawaii.[4]

Press comment on the Assembly recognized it as reflecting "the doubt and dissent" in the labor movement over the officialdom's "rock-solid support of the war in Vietnam," and as representing an important effort "to explore a more meaningful role for labor in the quest for peace." But none minimized the difficulties that still stood in the way of changing "the official AFL-CIO position." They pointed to a poll of delegates at 13 union conventions in October-November 1967 indicating overwhelming support for U.S. policy in Vietnam. The poll was conducted at AFL-CIO Committee on Political Education (COPE) booths at conventions or affiliated organizations in ten states. Of 3,542 delegates polled, 1,448 favored a continuation of U.S. policy, 1,368 favored escalation, 471 endorsed a policy of de-escalation and only 276 approved the idea of withdrawal. Yet those who pointed to these statistics conceded that it was difficult to tell how much the poll reflected rank-and-file opinion or that of the established labor leadership. Even the most skeptical of commentators agreed that the Labor Assembly for Peace indicated that a new wind was blowing in the labor movement, and that in view of the contradictions and tensions created by the war, a real possibility existed of building a strong minority opposition to it in the ranks of labor. But as for changing the basic policy of the AFL-CIO on the issue of Vietnam, both optimistic and pessimistic evaluations of the Labor Assembly were in agreement that this was not in the realm of an immediate possibility.

These estimates proved to be realistic. Meeting in Miami Beach on December 9, 1967, the AFL-CIO Executive Council once again reaffirmed the labor establishment's support of President Johnson's policies in Vietnam. (The vote was unanimous except for Jacob Potofsky, who abstained.) The seventh convention of the AFL-CIO opened at Bal Harbour, Florida, a month after the Labor Leadership Assembly. It quickly became clear that the AFL-CIO hierarchy was unwilling to concede an inch to the peace views expressed by the 523 trade unionists at Chicago. The usual support for the war was expressed, first, in the ovation tendered Dean Rusk after his speech defending it, and then in the warm reception President Johnson received in a personal appearance before the delegates to announce the beginning of his campaign for re-election and to praise them for their support of the war.

The only debate on the war was sparked when Charles Cogen, American Federation of Teachers president, urged the AFL-CIO to steer a neutral course in the national controversy over the Vietnam war. Acting as mandated by the national AFT convention in August 1967, Cogen took the floor with a substitute resolution calling on the AFL-CIO to take "no position on the Vietnam position."* Cogen spoke after Herman Kenin, president of the American Federation of Musicians, had introduced a resolution reaffirming the AFL-CIO's "unequivocal support of President Johnson's policy in

---

* The California Federation of Teachers, however, adopted a resolution at their convention in the fall of 1967 which denounced U.S. intervention, condemned the military escalation, and, after pointing out that as teachers and citizens they saw how the war was brutalizing the minds of American children and causing the abandonment of necessary domestic programs, called for immediate U.S. withdrawal.

Vietnam." Cogen told the 1,000 delegates: "there is a great division in the ranks of labor which we cannot disregard. In order to prevent further divisiveness which may develop, it is best for the AFL-CIO to take no position on this matter."

Cogen was followed by nine other delegates who spoke about Vietnam—two of whom opposed and seven of whom defended the U.S. policy in Vietnam. Leon Davis criticized the AFL-CIO arrangers for not scheduling dissenters on the Vietnam question to speak to delegates, and called the war a "tragic mistake." A. Toffoli of the Colorado State AFL-CIO council, addressing the convention as an individual, spoke about the Labor Leadership Assembly for Peace. While his references to Senator Eugene McCarthy and John Kenneth Galbraith as speakers at the Chicago conference drew choruses of boos from the delegates, he was able to read into the convention record the policy statement adopted by the Labor Leadership Assembly, thus bringing before the delegates the call for a halt in the bombing by the U.S. of North Vietnam and initiation by this country of a "sincere search for a negotiated peace settlement."

But this voice of sanity was drowned out by the succeeding speakers. Thomas Gleason, president of the International Longshoremen's Association, closed the debate on the proper pro-war note when he told the convention proudly: "We kept our muscles in shape all weekend in New York and we took care of those fellows that were burning their draft cards this last weekend in New York. We hope they will keep it up because we will just desecrate their ranks, if they have enough soldiers." This was greeted by cheers.

Before calling for a vote, Meany warned the convention not to be "isolationist" and denied that there was "division" on Vietnam in the labor movement. In reference to Toffoli's remarks on the Labor Leadership Assembly for Peace, Meany charged that the conference had been "planned in Hanoi by a special committee that went there," and that its statement critical of U.S. Vietnamese policy had been published two weeks in advance in the *Sunday Worker,* a Communist Party newspaper

—a statement that was pure fiction. He then went on to cite statistics which, he said, proved that union members approved of the Vietnam war by a margin of 600 to 1.

While there was no official tally of the number of votes on either side of the question on both Cogen's substitute resolution and the pro-war resolution, several newsmen covering the convention made estimates. The Washington *Post*'s reporter calculated that "among the 1,000-odd delegates an estimated 30 or 40, in a voice vote, backed Cogen's substitute." On a standing vote on the main resolution, backing Johnson's policy, the *New York Times*' reporter wrote that "only about a dozen of an estimated 1,200 delegates on the floor, rose to signify opposition."[5]

In Detroit Emil Mazey denounced Meany's statement as to the origin of the peace assembly and the printing of its resolution prior to the gathering as "libelous and slanderous, the kind you'd expect from a senile old man." But his words were never put into the convention's record. However, in an editorial on January 5, 1968, the *New York Times* sternly rebuked Meany and challenged his array of statistics:

> The finding of the last Gallup poll that unionists are quite evenly divided on how well President Johnson is handling the Vietnam war and on whether American troops should be fighting there at all indicates that, on this issue as on many others in the political realm, labor leaders are not always good barometers of the thinking of their members.
>
> At the Florida convention union officials who dissented from Administration policy were accused by George Meany of having plotted their strategy in Hanoi. The Gallup report should permit debate at future labor rallies to proceed without suggestions by Mr. Meany or anyone else that those who express doubts on the war felt by large numbers of American workers are automatically to be classified as enemy agents.

In a letter to "Dear George," published in *Labor Voice for Peace,* the official organ of the National Labor Leadership Assembly for Peace, Mazey quoted the

Times editorial. He pointed out that even after his "defamatory statements" about the Labor Peace Assembly had been proved false, Meany had continued to voice them, and he called upon the AFL-CIO president to make "a public retraction."[6]

As might be expected, Mazey's words were wasted on Meany. But the findings of the Gallup Poll, reported on January 3, 1968, indicating that almost one half of the rank and file of organized labor felt that the war was wrong, stimulated the groups set up by the Labor Assembly for Peace to continue its work and "encourage the formation of local Labor Leadership Assemblies in those areas where they do not already exist."[7] An Administrative Committee was established with Moe Foner, executive secretary of Local 1199, as national coordinator, and with the following members: Murray H. Finley, vice president and director, Midwest Joint Board, Amalgamated Clothing Workers; Stanley Greenspan, assistant director, International Affairs Department, United Auto Workers; Art Gundersheim, Education Department, Amalgamated Clothing Workers, Chicago, and David Livingston, president, District 65. The Administrative Committee published and distributed to trade unionists in over 40 cities 150,000 copies of *Labor Voice for Peace* containing excerpts from the proceedings of the Labor Assembly for Peace. At an all-day conference in Chicago, February 17, 1968, the 65-member Continuations Committee voted to make *Labor Voice for Peace* the official publication of the Assembly.

The January 22, 1968 issue of *Ford Facts*, official publication of the 45,000-member United Auto Workers Local 600 (the Ford local) featured the fact that one of the nation's biggest local unions had adopted the policy statement of the Labor Leadership Assembly for Peace and had also voted its own resolution on "Peace —The Only Alternative to Total Self-Destruction." The resolution called for an end to the war in Vietnam and included references to statements opposing the war by Pope Paul VI, U Thant, former U.S. Ambassador

George Kennan, and others. Copies were sent to the International Union, all members of Congress, Michigan State AFL-CIO and Wayne County AFL-CIO.

The older chapters of the Trade Union Division of SANE in New York City, Newark and other cities in New Jersey, Chicago, Cleveland, Detroit, Minneapolis, Los Angeles, San Francisco, Pittsburgh and Portland had reorganized themselves as chapters of the Labor Peace Assembly. New chapters were established in Milwaukee, Philadelphia, and Racine, Wisconsin.[8]

Even acknowledging its important contributions, one cannot escape the conclusion that the anti-war sentiment generated by the Labor Assembly for Peace seems to have had little lasting effect. Yet the course of events after November 1967 was extremely favorable for the growth of the Assembly's influence. The increase of the savage destruction of lives and villages in South Vietnam and the Tet offensive of the NLF in late January-February 1968, making it clear to those who once hoped for a speedy U.S. military victory that the war would drag on indefinitely, the mounting U.S. casualties, already surpassing Korea, the drafting of college graduates, and the mounting evidence that the drain on the nation's resources created by the war was making it impossible to meet the needs of the urban ghettos and other neglected sections of American society, had brought many new recruits into the peace movement. By March 1968, it was clear that a majority of the American people were opposed to the military-victory-at-any-price policy of the Johnson Administration. A Gallup Poll released on March 12 showed 69 per cent of those interviewed in favor of a pullout from Vietnam, and this included both "hawks" and "doves."[9]

Then came the stunning primary victory of Senator Eugene McCarthy in New Hampshire and the entrance into the Presidential nominations race of Senator Robert Kennedy, both running as peace candidates. Shortly thereafter came the announcement by President Johnson of his decision not to seek re-election in 1968, and the temporary halting of the bombing of North Vietnam.

Yet by the time of these events, it appears, only one additional union had been added to the list of those whose leaders had participated in the National Labor Leadership Assembly for Peace. This was Typographical Union No. 21 of San Francisco. After a campaign by a number of "Concerned Members of Local 21," including the issuance of a bulletin headed, "Speak Out! Union Printers Say 'No' to War," the local adopted a resolution in the spring of 1968 which stated: "We urge the President of the United States to immediately formulate a policy of peace in Vietnam and an orderly withdrawal from the present untenable position of the United States."[10]

The reasons for the failure of the National Labor Leadership Assembly for Peace are varied. Lack of funds undoubtedly hampered the ability of the Assembly to carry out the "ambitious program" set for it in January 1968.[11] Probably the fact that the NLLAP was primarily a movement of union functionaries and never reached down to the rank and file to any extent limited its effectiveness. But no doubt a major reason was the fact that the "stop the war movement" was advancing in a more radical direction than most trade unionists, including many of those who had been at Chicago, were prepared to go.

One must remember that the NLLAP grew out of the older and more established leadership of the organized anti-war protest, SANE. By the time the Labor Assembly came into being, this more respectable wing of the anti-war movement, with its emphasis upon peaceful protests such as meetings, marches and distribution of petitions, had already lost much of its influence and was being replaced by the radical elements of the New Left whose appeal was mainly to the youth. While SDS often stayed aloof from the peace forces until compelled to join, the New Left brought into the anti-war movement the confrontation tactics which had their origin in the Free Speech Movement at Berkeley in 1964 and spread during the next few years to many campuses—burning draft cards, obstructing Dow recruiters, confrontations with official spokesmen. As might be expected, the liberal, middle-class elements of the peace movement associated with SANE were soon alienated by the more radical tactics of the New Left. While Dr. Benjamin Spock, the co-chairman of SANE, felt that the peace movement had to encompass the more radical forces, his views were not shared by most of his colleagues.

The October 1967 anti-war demonstration in Washington provided clear evidence of the radicalization of the anti-war movement. While the majority of the 70,000 protesters were content to gather peacefully at the Lincoln Memorial, a few thousand, mainly young people associated with SDS radicals and Yippies, stormed the Pentagon. As they climbed the Pentagon walls, the troops tear-gassed and arrested many demonstrators. Many Americans overlooked the brutality of the troops and, influenced by the rage of the mass media against the demonstrators, were alienated by the confrontation tactics. To be sure, Dr. Spock in an interview over CBS the day after the storming of the Pentagon, declared: "I didn't find it distasteful myself, and I imagine that the majority of the American public would not find it distasteful."[12] It is doubtful if this was a correct estimate of public reaction.

It is significant that among the many speakers invited to address the Labor Peace Assembly in Chicago not a single student spokesman was included. Moreover, Mazey denounced the "flag burners," "VC flag carriers," and other tactics of the "lunatic fringe" of the anti-war movement as "playing into the hands of the Administration," and he warned that the UAW would not go along with any of it. This criticism of the anti-war Left did not sit too well with some of the delegates, but it was clear that if Mazey, the only delegate at the AFL-CIO convention at San Francisco in 1965 with the courage to rebuke Meany for his reference to the student peace protesters as "kookies," could go out of his way to criticize the tactics of the radical peace forces, the more cautious labor leaders would be very reluctant to align themselves with any anti-war movement more advanced and more radical than SANE.

In February 1968 the Labor Peace Assembly's Continuation Committee voted to encourage local chapters to cooperate with the campaign for a negotiated settlement of the war sponsored by Negotiations Now! But already the radical wing of the anti-war movement had only contempt for the Negotiations Now! demand and were willing to unite only with those demanding unilateral withdrawal of all American forces from Vietnam. This virtually guaranteed that even the labor leaders who had spoken out against the war would not be part of an anti-war movement with so advanced a program; but it did not bother a major section of the anti-war Left. Many spokesmen for the New Left saw no distinction among labor leaders or differentiation in the trade unions. To them Mazey, Gorman, Victor Reuther, and most of the other labor leaders associated with the peace assembly were no different than Meany. The fact that these leaders had broken with Meany over Vietnam and had begun to mobilize a strong minority in the AFL-CIO against the Meany-Lovestone forces made not the slightest difference to significant New Left elements. Many among them, with little direct knowledge of labor's problems, had long since written off the labor movement as a meaningful ally in any movement which aimed to change conditions in the United States, especially to change American foreign policy.

In the spring of 1968 the peace movement turned political, challenging the Democratic Party in various communities. It found itself without the backing of labor, including the forces associated with the Assembly for Peace. Many of the anti-war labor leaders were still linked to the Democratic machine. Though Victor Reuther and Mazey had both spoken at the Assembly for Peace in Chicago, though the huge Ford local had endorsed the Assembly's policy statement, few labor people expressed interest in the peace candidates of the Michigan Conference of Concerned Democrats or even in Eugene V. McCarthy. The Michigan McCarthy chairman put it bluntly in March 1968: "We can't expect much help from labor."[13]

The leaders of the Labor Assembly for Peace hailed

McCarthy's victory in New Hampshire, but they did not urge its chapters to work for his candidacy. Perhaps they realized that just as many militant New Left groups were dissatisfied with McCarthy's moderate proposals to de-escalate the war, organized labor found him too indifferent to issues other than Vietnam to be to their liking. At any rate, it was the "children's crusade," the anti-war students who worked tirelessly for his candidacy, not the labor peace forces, that made McCarthy's primary victories possible. "We don't have much support from organized labor," McCarthy himself acknowledged early in April.[14]

Robert Kennedy, as might be expected, had much greater support among trade unionists. Had he not been tragically assassinated, it is likely that the peace forces in the labor movement would have rallied to his support at the Chicago convention, even though the AFL-CIO leadership, which regretted Johnson's abdication perhaps more than anyone else in the Democratic Party machine, had endorsed Hubert Humphrey. Moreover, the United Auto Workers had by now left the AFL-CIO, regarding it, in the words of Walter Reuther, as "too fat, too complacent, too far out of touch with changing times." While the 1.6-million-worker union had been neutral in the primaries, it was leaning toward Kennedy at the time of his death. But even Kennedy had discovered that in important states with prime defense contracts, it was not easy to arouse labor interest in a Vietnam peace policy which, as they saw it, would affect wartime prosperity, bringing a reduction of billions in defense spending and a drop in manufacturing employment.[15]

The labor peace forces were not present at the great confrontation of anti-war groups in Chicago at the time of the Democratic convention. The brutal events that accompanied this dramatic episode brought little response from the labor movement other than a rebuke of Mayor Daley's police from Walter Reuther. Meany, of course, praised the police.[16]

The war in Vietnam had triggered among students a disenchantment with America over a wide variety of issues. The radical student movement had gone from seeking to revolutionize the university to revolutionizing government and society. The events in Chicago—the callous rejection by the Democratic machine of a meaningful peace platform and the brutal police actions—had caused further radicalization of the youth. But these actions had increased the hostility of many white trade unionists toward the radical youth. White members of Ford Local UAW in Detroit, interviewed by the *New York Times* in September, told of their decision to vote for Wallace for President, and explained that the Alabama racist governor's stand in favor of the war, against more freedom for blacks, and especially his call for a tough attitude toward youth demonstrators and the restoration of "law and order" had brought them to this decision.[17]

As the campaign drew to a close, the unions succeeded in convincing such workers that a vote for Wallace would be against their own interest since the Alabamian's record as governor proved he was an "enemy of labor." But to most observers it appeared that the distance between the radical youth and the trade unionists was impossible to bridge, and that an alliance between them to achieve change in American society and especially an end to the war in Vietnam was utterly out of the question. This was a premature judgment.

4

DIVISION DEEPENS

WHEN NIXON ASSUMED THE PRESIDENCY IN JANUARY 1969, THE PEACE MOVEMENT WAS IN DISARRAY. To Washington's surprise, North Vietnam had responded quickly and affirmatively to President Johnson's call for negotiations at the time he announced his decision not to seek re-election, accepting the partial bombing halt as an adequate basis for preliminary talks. Negotiations had gotten under way in Paris, and Johnson had ordered a total bombing halt in October. During the campaign Nixon had put himself on record as believing that there could be no military solution in Vietnam and had promised to end America's military presence in that country if elected, although he refused to spell out any specific plan for achieving that goal. The general feeling in the country as he assumed office was that of "wait and see" while giving the new President a chance to fulfill his campaign pledge.

But there were still 550,000 American troops in Vietnam; American dead were still running between 200 and 400 a week; the war was still costing $30 billion a year; the cost of living was still rising month after month, and the domestic ills of America were increasingly crying out for solution. It was inevitable, therefore, that the protest movement would come alive again and demand an end to an immoral national policy which continued to send Americans to be killed in support of a corrupt regime in Saigon and squandered the nation's wealth and energy in an unjust war while claiming there were no means to end poverty, disease, hunger and racism at home. When it did reassert itself, the peace movement would involve more trade union support than ever before.

How then does one explain the close links that developed between the peace forces and the labor movement during the Nixon Administration? The once monolithic stand of the AFL-CIO on the war issue had already been broken with the formation of the National Labor Leadership Assembly for Peace. This trend continued when the Reuther group took the UAW out of the AFL-CIO. Then in June 1969 the Teamsters and the Auto Workers met in Washington at a two-day convention and formed the Alliance for Labor Action. The proceedings of this meeting of 500 delegates from the two largest and most powerful unions in America revealed that the peace movement had gained a most valuable ally. Delegate after delegate spoke out against the Vietnam war, the military-industrial complex, and the ABM system. Frank Fitzimmons, who had assumed leadership of the Teamsters after James Hoffa had been sent to jail, delivered a bitter attack on the war in Vietnam, saying bluntly: "This war, the bane and plague of both Democratic and Republican administrations, must be stopped and must be stopped soon. If it is not, its consequence will tear the fabric of America until there is serious doubt that the tear can be mended satisfactorily." Fitzimmons went even further, announcing a new approach by labor to the youth movement:

I for one do not believe that the so-called generation gap is something which cannot be bridged. I believe that a constructive and meaningful dialogue can be established with the youngsters if we only take time to talk to them. Just standing back and shaking our heads when they storm a university or when they demonstrate is not enough.

Einar Mohn, West Coast Teamster leader, followed with a moving speech in which he criticized the labor movement for not understanding youth and not doing much in the battle against discrimination: He called for more than resolutions in favor of "equal opportunities and equal rights for Americans," warning that unless the unions did something concrete to train "young blacks and browns" and open up jobs and membership, "then we are in trouble." Regarding the youth, he reminded the union delegates:

I don't believe in violence on the campus, but why do we get so thin-skinned? I remember when it was a high insurance risk to cross a picket line to scab. I also remember a city on the Great Lakes where union members took over buildings illegally for many days. We often here offer platitudes to the younger generation today. We should realize that 50 per cent of them in the next period will be ours, and we've got to help them. And one way to help them is to try to understand.

The ALA's declaration of purposes, adopted unanimously, urged an immediate end to the war in Vietnam, and announced the determination of the new labor body to unite with all peace forces in achieving this objective and "to develop policies and carry out programs that will enable the American labor movement to repair the alienation of the liberal-intellectual and academic community and the youth of our nation in order to build and strengthen a new alliance of progressive forces in the broad effort to advance the common good."[1]

While the New Left by and large viewed the proceedings in Washington as "just talk," many in the peace movement were not slow to see the implications of the ALA policy stand. They would not have been surprised to hear that Reuther or Mazey of the UAW or even Harold Gibbons, the foremost intellectual in the Teamsters, had spoken out against the war, the military-industrial complex, and the escalation of the arms race. But when the leaders of the Teamsters, who epitomized the image of organized labor's lack of concern with anything but practical issues like more wages and shorter hours, came out strongly against the war and in favor of a new foreign policy, then indeed it would appear that an important section of the labor movement was ready to lend its strength to the fight against the war. To this should be added the fact that here was an organization with the economic, political and financial power to make its influence felt.

The ALA position was only one sign of a whole series of changes which had been occurring in the labor movement and which reached their climax during the Nixon Administration. For several years big business had been discovering that the value of trade unions as "managers of discontent" (a description coined by C. Wright Mills in his book *New Men of Power,* published in 1948) was diminishing. For one thing, revolts against old bureaucrats had led to the replacement of David McDonald, James Carey, George Burdon, and O. A. Knight by new leaders. While the new leaders were not too different from their predecessors, their election came as a surprise to those who had no inkling of the widespread rank-and-file unrest in the unions.

Another clear sign of this unrest was the report in the February 9, 1967 issue of the *Wall Street Journal* that union members in 1966 rejected 11.7 per cent of all settlements participated in by the government's Federal Mediation Conciliation Service. By the beginning of 1969, even labor leaders were talking of the "alienated rank and file" and what was termed "the rejection syndrome" —the growing tendency of the rank and file to reject contracts that had been negotiated by the officers. This tendency, reported Damon Stetson in the *New York Times,* reflects "a spirit of rebellion against the Establishment that seems to have become epidemic."[2] The growing incidence of wildcat strikes and rejection of recommended contract settlements testified to the fact that a revolt was already under way against a mountain of grievances, many of which had been festering for years. The rank-and-file workers were tired of being robbed of their wages by constantly rising prices and an unjust tax system, of speedup and other dangerous working conditions, and, in the case of black workers, of discrimination on jobs and racist union practices as well. They were tired, too, of an authoritarian, despotic union leadership that was indifferent to their needs, and they were demanding a more direct voice in decisions affecting their welfare.[3]

The peace movement was well aware of the fact that the rank-and-file revolt in the labor movement did not include the demand to "end the war now" in its objectives. But it was obvious that the discontent already revealed in the ranks of organized labor presented a potentially important recruiting ground for the anti-war movement. The main task was to convince the rank-and-file workers that the Vietnam war was closely related to their discontent: that it was the war which was the major cause of inflation, and while it brought enormous profits to the big corporations, it was bringing exorbitant prices and outrageous taxes to the working people, and that the very same labor leaders who dragged their feet in fighting to improve the conditions of the rank and file were also the staunchest supporters of the war. In short, it was necessary to puncture the view so long cherished by many workers that as long as the war continued, their conditions would be better and better. This was an illusion. With inflation wiping out the savings of many workers and even requiring a goodly number to hold two or three jobs to make ends meet, it had to be made clear to them that the argument that the war was a blessing to the working class was so much nonsense.

Simultaneous with the changes occurring in the labor movement came a change in the character of the peace-movement and the outlook of many in the radical youth movement. In 1969 the New Mobilization Committee to End the War in Vietnam was organized by a group of anti-war protesters, including many former workers for Senator McCarthy. The Committee believed that a successful anti-war strategy had to include those Americans who while opposed to the war were not ready to accept the tactics of the anti-war Left. Moreover, they rejected the view of the New Left that there was no difference between Meany and Reuther and did not dismiss the entire labor movement as too corrupted to be an ally in the anti-war struggle. On the contrary, New Mobe (as the Committee was called) established a Trade Union Committee, headed by Sidney Lens and Stewart Meacham. The NMC offered its help in building trade union committees to end the war.

Quite a number of radical students, too, were beginning to have second thoughts about the correctness of ignoring the working class in the movement to end the war. This section of the radical youth movement had finally come to the realization that while students could protest and should continue to do so, they did not have the power to force a real change in policy. The working class was the key to achieving this objective. As a leaflet jointly distributed by the SDS Labor Committee, International Socialists, Columbia Student Mobilization Committee, and Columbia Young Socialist Alliance put it:

Almost everyone in the anti-war movement recognizes that students alone do not have the power to end the war in Vietnam. Essentially this is because as a group in society they do not contribute anything to the continuation of the war. This certainly does not mean that students should not continue to build mass demonstrations against the war. In fact students should step up their efforts and attempt to involve all sectors of society in the anti-war movement.

The leaflet called upon students, if they really wanted to end the war, to "seek to unite with those who have the power to do so," and foremost among those were the workers.[4] "Build ties with the workers," became a leading cry of this section of the radical youth movement.

During 1969 these students brought their action into line with their rhetoric. They joined picket lines of strikers and showed their solidarity with them in other ways. Their offers of help were often nullified by a tendency to tell workers how to run their strikes and just as often rejected by strikers who felt that "hippies" hurt rather than helped their cause. But not infrequently the students were welcomed and student-labor cooperation got under way. A pioneer step in "worker-student alliance" was taken in the San Francisco area early in 1969 when there were simultaneous strikes by oil workers at Standard Oil in Richmond and by students (led by a Black Students Union and a Third World Liberation Front) and teachers at San Francisco State College. At a joint press conference announcing the alliance of refinery and campus strikers, G. T. Jacobs, secretary-treasurer of Oil, Chemical and Atomic Workers, Local 1–561, declared: "It is not just police brutality that unites us. We are all exploited, black workers more than white, but we all have the same enemy, the big corporations. And it is corporations, like our enemy, Standard Oil, that control the Board of Trustees of the state colleges the students are fighting."[5]

During the 100-day strike of 150,000 electrical workers against General Electric's policy of Boulwarism—the policy ordering workers to take or leave the company's offer—students supported the all-union boycott of GE products, collected money and food for the strikers, and demanded that university administrators halt GE recruiting on campuses. Their leaflets pointed out that GE, as the second largest defense contractor, was a major part of the military-industrial complex.

For its part, the New Mobe called upon the Senate to investigate General Electric's use of profits made in the Vietnam war to break the strike. It pointed out that one-fifth of GE's total business was in war contracts, and that its profits from these contracts and its cheap-labor plants in Southeast Asia helped GE resist the demands of the unions.[6]

These efforts of the peace organizations and the radical students to build ties with working people brought significant results not only in contributing to the victory of the GE and other strikers but also in building antiwar sentiment in the working class. Moratorium Day, October 15, 1969, offered visible proof. A full-page ad in major newspapers calling for the Moratorium included the names of Paul Schrade, Western Director of the UAW, and Cesar Chavez, Director of the United Farm Workers. Large ads were also run in many papers by the three unions associated in the Alliance for Labor Action signed by Walter Reuther for the UAW, Frank E. Fitzsimmons and Thomas E. Flynn for the Teamsters, and Thomas E. Boyle and Marshall Shafer for the Chemical Workers. Headed, "We Take Our Stand for Peace and an End to the War in Vietnam," the ad called upon the government "to face up to the reality that there is nothing to be won in Vietnam that is worth one more drop of American blood." Emphasizing that "Peace Can Unite America to Wage War Against Poverty, Hunger, Ignorance and Disease," the ad called fur-

After the attacks by hard tops on peace demonstrators in New York, Walter Stack, a hodcarrier, rode up and down the length of Market Street, a main thoroughfare in San Francisco, with a sign proclaiming "HARD HATS NOT ALL STORMTROOPERS."— *From the* Chronicle, *June 10, 1970.*

ther for bringing the troops home and putting "the sad Vietnamese chapter of our history behind us."

Among the millions of Americans who came together on that historic Wednesday, in answer to the call of the Vietnam Moratorium Committee, endorsed by numerous organizations including trade unions, to petition their government to end the Vietnam war, were the thousands of union members who had previously been involved in marching in the streets, signing petitions, and making their opposition to the war public in other ways. But the greatest war protest in American history also brought out hundreds of thousands of trade unionists who had never before been associated with the anti-war movement. In New York City alone some 40 trade unions announced their support of the Moratorium. Demonstrations were held in union shops, hospitals and nursing homes; unionists carried signs reading, "Peace Now!" "Peace Action Day!" "Make Health Not War!" and "Our Boys Mean More Than Our Pride!" Tens of thousands in Detroit heard Douglas Fraser, UAW Chrysler director, Myra Wolfgang of the Hotel and Restaurant Workers Union, and Grady Glenn, president, Frame Building, Ford Local 600. In Los Angeles, Paul Schrade, UAW Executive Board member said that October 15th was "only the beginning of labor's involvement in the anti-war movements."[7]

AFL-CIO and ALA unionists demonstrated together and speakers from both organizations shared the platform. The AFL-CIO unionists acted in the face of the continued support of the Nixon Administration's war policy by the top leadership. Hardly two weeks before the Moratorium, Meany re-stated at the AFL-CIO convention his support of the war, although he conceded for the first time that it was "unpopular." He criticized those demanding withdrawal from Vietnam for creating obstacles to a negotiated settlement, and charged that they were "in fact encouraging those on the other side of the table not to negotiate."[8]

Before the Moratorium President Nixon had said that he would not be swayed by the demonstrations for "Peace Now!" This unprecedented act of indifference by a President to the wishes of millions of the nation's citizens had the effect of strengthening the anti-war movement which announced plans for a march on Washington, November 15. Immediately many trade unions began to mobilize their membership to take part. In Chicago, Patrick Gorman called a citywide meeting of labor representatives to prepare for November 15th. The Labor Committee of the Detroit Coalition to End the War Now distributed a leaflet signed by a partial list of over 200 trade union officials and members calling upon workers and citizens to join them "in making the Nov. 15th moratorium to bring the GI's home, a million people demonstration." Among the sponsors were: Harold J. Gibbons, international vice president, International Brotherhood of Teamsters; Tom Posler, president, International Association of Firefighters Local 1279, AFL-CIO; John Grindstaff, president, American Federation of Teachers, Local 1465, AFL-CIO; three vice presidents of the Michigan Federation of Teachers, and scores of presidents, committeemen, shop stewards, shop committeemen of the United Auto Workers and other unions. It was headed, "Labor Says: 'End the War!' " and carried the following message:

Workers are paying the cost of the war in Vietnam. This disastrous, costly and racist war is killing our sons, taxing hell out of our paychecks and sucking up the rest in high prices.

The five million member Alliance for Labor Action (UAW, Teamsters and Chemical Workers) is backing the anti-war movement. Its leaders, Walter Reuther, Frank Fitzsimmons and Thomas Boyle are speaking out.

The ALA stated: "We call upon our government to face up to the reality that there is nothing to be won in Vietnam that is worth one drop of American blood. The only question remaining is not *whether* we will withdraw our troops but *how* and *when*. We take our stand with those who are for getting out quickly and completely. . . . It has become increasingly clear that national priorities have been seriously distorted, that too much of budgets has been diverted to military purposes, while human needs have been neglected."[9]

On the West Coast, too, unions organized for November 15th. *El Malcriado* (the Voice of the Farm Worker), organ of the United Farm Workers Organizing Committee, engaged in the historic campaign to organize the Mexican-Americans (Chicanos) and other farm workers and gain union recognition from the table grape growers of California, devoted several pages of its November 1969 issue to the anti-war demonstration and urged all Chicanos to participate. It cited a recent survey which had revealed that 20 per cent of the casualties from five Southwestern states in Vietnam were Chicanos even though persons with Spanish surnames, as demonstrated in a study by Dr. Ralph Gurzman of the University of California at Santa Cruz, made up only 10 per cent of the population in these states. *El Malcriado* noted that since a very small percentage of Chicanos are financially able to attend college—less than 10 per cent of the 97,000 University of California students were Chicanos—they are excluded from student deferments. The same explanation, of course, applied to casualties of blacks in Vietnam.

The San Francisco-Bay Area Labor Assembly for Peace sent a mailing to some 1,000 local unions in northern California, urging them to support the March and enclosing a leaflet especially directed to the effects of the war on trade unions. The leaflet included the six national demands: (1) immediate and total withdrawal from Vietnam; (2) a halt to ABM construction and increasing militarism; (4) self-determination for Vietnam and black and minority people in America; (5) an end to political repression and freedom for all political prisoners; and (6) constitutional rights for GI's.

Tens of thousands of trade unionists marched down Pennsylvania Avenue to the Washington Monument on November 15. The meeting at the Monument featured Gibbons of the Teamsters; Gorman and Rosenblum sent messages of support. On the West Coast the Labor Assembly for Peace led unionists from the International Longshoremen's and Warehousemen's, Painters, Communication Workers, Transport Workers, and Teachers in parade. Paul Schrade, vice president of the UAW and Dolores Huerta, vice president of the United Farm Workers Organizing Committee, represented labor on the platform.

Like Moratorium Day, the November 15th demonstrations revealed a growing unity of labor and peace forces. It was this important development in the antiwar movement which caused Deputy Attorney General Kleindienst to announce an investigation of the New Mobilization Committee, sponsors of the October and November demonstrations. Labor replied immediately. John Sheehan, legislative Director of the United Steel Workers, said, "This threat to investigate the peace movement is very ominous. It smacks of McCarthyism. The Justice Department is attempting to destroy opposition through investigation. . . . The mood of the country is different today. The people will slap this down before it gets very far." Paul Wagner, legislative director of the UAW, said, "The Justice Department is pulling out the script of the Fifties a la Joe McCarthy."[10]

The discussion of the war made its way into the leading labor papers. The *Missouri Teamster* for January 1970 published a summary of the speech delivered by Vice President Gibbons on Moratorium Day. Gibbons called the work of those helping to disengage the United States from Vietnam, "An act of the highest patriotism and a distinct service to our country." On February 16, Gibbons announced to the Teamsters Joint Council in St. Louis, which he headed, that the *Missouri Teamster* would run a discussion on the Vietnam war issue. In a message to the council's members, Gibbons noted that after his Moratorium Day activities and speech in Washington, "some of our members agree with this position; some disagree." This was "perfectly understandable," he wrote, and he observed that "unfortunately those who dissent from our national policies in Vietnam have too often been treated with suppression or accused of a lack of patriotism." He then proposed that the pages of the *Missouri Teamster* provide a forum for views on the issue "pro and con."

Summarizing his own position, Gibbons wrote that he deplored the "reprehensible activities of a small minority," who burn the American flag or others who equate anti-Americanism with anti-war. The effect of their work was "counter-productive." But he went on to de-

clare again his belief that the "support of efforts to disengage America from Vietnam is an act of the highest
patriotism and a distinct service to our country."[11]

That Gibbons spoke for a wide section of American
labor leadership became clear on February 25. On that
day the Washington *Post* carried a full page ad signed
by 123 unionists, including the leaders of 22 unions,
who declared, "We urge all trade unionists to join with
their fellow Americans to demand an immediate withdrawal of troops and cessation of hostilities in Vietnam,
and to begin putting our money where it counts—at
home." The ad was dominated by a picture of a GI with
the slogan, "War is hell," written across his helmet. A
banner headline read, "A rich man's war and a poor
man's fight." "Hawk or dove, we are all clay pigeons," it
continued. The statement closed:

> As long as we are in Vietnam we will have insufficient
> housing, education and health care. Our cities will rot.
> We cannot and will not have both guns and butter.
> Vietnam is eating up the money that is desperately needed
> for domestic programs. Compared with other federal ex-
> penditures during the last 10 fiscal years the Vietnam war
> has cost ten times more than Medicare, 16 times more than
> Aid to Education, 33 times more than Housing and Com-
> munity Development, 18 times more than the War on
> Poverty.

This declaration was signed by more trade unionists
and included more trade unions than any previous labor
manifesto against the war. The sponsor of the ad was
the Labor Peace Committee, co-chaired by Anthony
Mazzocchi, Roy Morgan and Marvin Rogoff, representing the AFL-CIO and the Alliance for Labor Action.
Signers, mostly labor officials, included Victor Reuther
and Russell Leach, the latter executive director of the
Alliance for Labor, but many AFL-CIO unionists were
represented. The unions represented included:

> United Auto Workers, International Brotherhood of Team-
> sters, Alliance for Labor Action, Amalgamated Meat
> Cutters and Butcher Workmen, Oil, Chemical and Atomic
> Workers, American Federation of Musicians, American
> Federation of State, County and Municipal Workers,

American Federation of Teachers, American Federation of Technical Engineers, American Newspaper Guild, Communication Workers of America, Hotel and Restaurant Workers, International Association of Machinists, International Longshoremen and Warehousemen's Union, International Union of Electrical, Radio and Machine Workers, Laborers International Union of North America, National Federation of Social Service Employees, Office and Professional Employees International Union, Retail Clerks International Association, Service Employees International Union, and the United Farm Workers Organizing Committee.

Several of these unions had been involved in previous anti-war activity, but the significant fact was that the majority had heretofore not joined any peace movement or expressed public opposition to the war. Moreover, several of the unions represented had been in the forefront of the labor supporters of the AFL-CIO's cold-war foreign policy. Unions which had been expelled from the CIO for having opposed this policy were now united with organizations which had voted for the expulsion.

The theme of the advertisement reflected the new emphasis of the peace movement in protesting the economic hardships caused by the war in Vietnam. Many workers had been horrified, along with most Americans, by the barbaric massacre at Songmy, and had reacted with anger as they saw on television the pictures of the atrocities committed by U.S. soldiers in cold-bloodedly killing hundreds of South Vietnamese men, women and children. The atrocities certainly contributed to their feeling that the United States had no business in Vietnam and that it should get out as fast as the ships and planes could bring the soldiers home. But more effective in causing them to reach this conclusion was the fact that living costs and rising taxes were wiping out all gains won at the bargaining table, and that overtime and the holding of two jobs, the only way in which workers had heretofore been able to keep their heads above water, was disappearing in the economic slowdown already under way.

Statistics published by analysts bore out what every worker already knew from his daily experience. Labor pacts negotiated in 1969 won workers median wage increases of 8 per cent. In hourly terms, contracts through the first 11 months of 1969 averaged increases of 22.2 cents, according to the Bureau of National Affairs, up from 18.4 cents a year earlier. But although gross average weekly earnings of workers climbed from $103.47 at year end 1967 to $117.25 in 1969, in 1957–59 dollars the increase represented an improvement of less than $2 a week—from $87.77 to $89.30—and this with overtime. The rise of 11 per cent in consumer prices had eaten up the gains obtained through negotiations. By the spring of 1970, in the New York-Northeastern New Jersey area, the average factory production worker's pay check had gone up in dollars but had lost 3.9 per cent in buying power in the two years, including 1.9 per cent in 1969 alone. The Federal Bureau of Labor Statistics which released this information reported on May 5, 1970 that "real spendable earnings" in the area were down $3.30 a week in the two-year period, including a loss of $1.62 in the last year. Herbert Bienstock, the Bureau's regional director, acknowledged that "inflation has played havoc with wage gains in recent years." The gross pay check for factory production workers in the area averaged $131.43 in March 1970, but buying power for such a worker with three dependents was only $82.01, measured in terms of what dollars were worth during the 1957–59 period.[12]

No one should have been surprised that 1970 saw an enormous increase in strikes, especially wildcat and runaway strikes, and an unprecedented rise in the rejection of contracts drawn up between industry and labor leaders. The Nixon Administration's pious pleas that labor exercise restraint at the bargaining table sounded hollow when it continued to pour billions into the war—the primary cause of inflation; $8.9 million was still being expended on artillery shells and bombs in Vietnam in a single day!

Rank-and-file teamsters rejected an inadequate contract negotiated by their leaders. Teachers all over the country went on strike and faced injunctions, fines and jail. Postal workers went on strike for the first time in

195 years, over the opposition of their leaders. In the face of government threats, military strike-breaking, and foot-dragging union leaders, and even though they knew they were risking their jobs, security, and pensions, some 200,000 postal workers held firm to the demand for a wage increase.

The postal strikers received the support of the peace movement and many of the radical students, who had already decided that no fundamental change in American society, including its foreign policy, was possible to achieve without the power of the working class. (The breakdown of the normal functioning of the country, especially the industrial, commercial, and financial sectors, during the postal strike lent considerable weight to this argument.) On March 19, 1970 the Trade Union Committee of the New Mobe sent Postmaster General Winton Blount the following telegram:

The New Mobilization Committee to End the War in Vietnam speaks for millions of Americans who oppose the war in Vietnam and Laos and wish to advise you of its full support for the striking postal workers in the New York area. It is a mockery of all human decency that a nation which spends 30 billion dollars on an illegal and immoral war, refuses to find a pittance to provide a living wage to underpaid letter carriers. As concerned citizens we demand that you cancel war expenditures and turn from life destroying to life fulfilling efforts. We demand you meet in full the postal employees' requests.[13]

Despite the mountains of evidence pointing up the disastrous effect the war had on the living standards of millions of workers and its responsibility for increasing the ills of American society, the anti-war movement subsided in the winter and early spring of 1970. The great mass of the American people had demonstrated on October 15 and again on November 15, 1969 that they wanted peace. But many had been taken in by Nixon's "Vietnamization" speech of November 3. According to this plan, presented on the eve of the great anti-war demonstration planned for Washington on November 15, the Saigon armed forces would be upgraded and American manpower in Vietnam reduced by stages until the point would be reached that there would be few Americans fighting in that country. As "Vietnamization" proceeded, the North Vietnamese would see the necessity of negotiating a settlement on American terms.

The peace movement rejected "Vietnamization" as a device to defuse anti-war protests while at the same time pursuing the goal of military victory in Vietnam. The idea that the army of a corrupt, dictatorial clique in Saigon could be turned into a force capable of coping with the toughest, most experienced liberation fighters in Asia was termed either self-delusion or a trick to pull the wool over the eyes of the American people. Moreover, "Vietnamization" would only mean the continuation of the destruction of Vietnam, with Asians killing Asians, while American imperialism picked up the pieces. However one analyzed the Nixon Administration's Vietnam policy—and as on most issues it kept contradicting itself—it all added up to the indefinite continuation of a detestable war.

But many Americans bought the President's rhetoric, and throughout the winter and early spring of 1970, it looked as though Nixon's tactics were succeeding in neutralizing anti-war sentiment. Still anti-war protests continued. April 1970 Vietnam Moratorium Observances began with a Fast for Peace. On April 13 trade unionists and businessmen in Washington fasted at a "non-banquet" set up in Lafayette Park across from the White House. The 200 war protesters sat at banquet tables set for a luncheon but only a glass of water was served. William Simon, black president of the Washington local of the American Federation of Teachers, told the anti-war fasters: "Maybe some day someone across the street will have guts enough to admit this war was a mistake."

Henry Niles, chairman of Business Executives Move for Peace, read a statement agreed to by the Washington Labor for Peace Committee and his organization which declared: "The war is killing our sons, destroying our economy, raising our taxes and neglecting our cities. This senseless war must be ended."[14]

April 15 was designated by the Vietnam Moratorium Committee as a day of demonstrations against the rising burden of war taxes, paid particularly by working people, and the war-caused inflation. Peace and labor forces were urged to unite to demonstrate outside offices of the Internal Revenue Bureau to end the war-tax and war-inflation by ending the war. A number of demonstrations, with trade unions represented, did take place. But they were disappointingly small compared with the November 15 turn-out.

Still the evidence pointed to the fact that anti-war sentiment had not ceased to grow in extent and intensity. The Gallup Poll issued on April 11, 1970 revealed that public confidence in Nixon's Vietnam policies had declined steadily since January, with less than half of all adults interviewed in the survey expressing approval of the policy.[15] More significant was the publication of an article in *Dissent* entitled, "Dove Sentiment Among Blue-Collar Workers." Harlan Hahan, the author, noted that "Several studies of public attitudes have demonstrated that persons with meager incomes or limited education are more likely than those of higher status to oppose the escalation of the war and to support a withdrawal of U.S. troops from Vietnam." He pointed out further that studies of local referendums held on the Vietnam war supported this finding in public opinion polls, and that *"the . . . vote against the war in nearly every referendum was concentrated in working-class rather than in upper-class segments of the communities."*

The studies referred to had been conducted by professional sociologists and political scientists since 1964 and every one of them had found that the greatest support for escalating the war came from those with yearly incomes in excess of $10,000, while the greatest degree of support for complete withdrawal of all U.S. troops from Vietnam came from people who had never finished high school and whose yearly incomes were below $5,000. These findings had been confirmed in the Gallup Poll Index, Reports No. 40 and No. 49, which showed that people with high incomes, a good deal of formal education and in high-status occupations, were in favor of escalation of the war, while those with low incomes, little schooling and with "low-status" occupations, and particularly, blue-collar workers, were increasingly hostile to the continuation of the war. The national surveys had been confirmed by local studies such as those of Detroit in 1966, of Cambridge and Lincoln, Massachusetts in 1968, of Dearborn, Michigan in 1968, and of San Francisco, and Madison, Wisconsin in 1967–1968. Altogether they presented a picture of deep opposition to the war in the working class, particularly the blue-collar workers.[16]

The evidence that the workers had consistently shown the greatest opposition to the war and had cast the highest percentage of votes in referendums against it gave the lie to the argument of Meany and his cohorts on the AFL-CIO Executive Council that workers, by and large, were in favor of the war and endorsed the unchanging support the AFL-CIO leadership had given to the policy of escalation. It also gave the lie to the charge, often voiced in the mass media, that the labor groups which had spoken out in favor of U.S. withdrawal from Vietnam were only a few pacifists or ideologically committed radicals who represented no one but themselves. Still only a few read *Dissent* and the articles by Martin Patchen, Richard F. Hamilton, Jerome Skolnick, Victoria Bonnell, Chester Hartman and Albert Sugarman in such publications as *Social Problems, American Sociological Review,* and *War/Peace Report.* The myth, still popular in some radical circles, that American workers had been bribed into supporting the war by jobs financed out of the military budget, persisted. It was soon to be shattered.

In April 1970 the anti-war movement was in a state of quiescence. It was the calm before the storm.

5

CAMBODIA: INITIAL RESPONSE

ON APRIL 29, 1970, PRESIDENT NIXON ANNOUNCED THE AMERICAN INVASION OF CAMBODIA OSTENSIBLY to destroy Vietcong and North Vietnamese bases in that country. The following day the United States bombed North Vietnam. Simultaneously with his escalation of the war in Indochina, the President escalated his attacks on student protesters. His reference to "bums," on top of Vice President Agnew's repeated attacks on anti-war protesters as "traitors," contributed to the mood in which National Guardsmen murdered four white students and wounded ten more at Kent State University. On the heels of the shootings at Kent came the murder by state police of six blacks in Augusta, Georgia, and the brutal slaying by Mississippi police of two black students at Jackson State, Mississippi.

The Nixon Administration's widening of the war it had promised to end and the slaying of the students—more so the whites at Kent State than the blacks at Jackson State—produced a tidal wave of protest unprecedented in American history. Angry and anguished citizens from all walks of life stood up to say "End the war" and "Stop the murders and repression at home." Strike actions of one sort or another broke out at hundreds of colleges and universities, in the biggest and most prestigious institutions, small colleges, even those hitherto regarded as immune against demonstrations, and at innumerable secondary schools. Almost every newspaper acknowledged that the Cambodian invasion and the killing of the Kent students a few days after the invasion began had brought the nation to its most critical point since the Civil War.

Cambodia produced a reaction from trade unionists which was both greater and qualitatively different from that which had followed previous crises of the Vietnam war. It brought into the anti-war movement huge sections of the trade unions never before involved in such protests, and produced a more advanced anti-war stand from the labor movement than heretofore. It also brought direct participation of many rank-and-file workers into anti-war activities for the first time.

However, whereas in the academic community there were few students who spoke out in favor of Nixon's war policies, the situation was quite different in the labor movement. The reaction of some sections of the trade unions—those symbolizing the hard-hat syndrome —to the President's escalation of the war was to intensify their pro-war activities. In short, the invasion of Cambodia and the events that followed directly afterward both multiplied many times the number of opponents of the war in the labor movement and at the same time sharpened past divisions on the war within organized labor.

The afternoon after the President spoke, two statements indicated the division in the labor movement on the invasion of Cambodia. Speaking in Arizona, Joseph Beirne, president of the Communications Workers and an AFL-CIO vice president, warned workers not to join the rising protest movement. This would be, he insisted, against their own interests since it would only lead to widespread unemployment. He put it bluntly:

Suppose last night, instead of escalating into Cambodia, President Nixon said we are pulling every man out in the quickest manner, with airplanes and ships; if he had said that last night, this morning the Pentagon would have notified thousands of companies, and said "your contract is cancelled"; by tomorrow millions would be laid off. The effect of our war, while it is going on, is to keep an economic pipeline loaded with a turnover of dollars because people are employed in manufacturing the things of war. If you ended that, tomorrow these same people wouldn't start making houses.[1]

It is not without significance that the first public defense of President Nixon's invasion of Cambodia came from a trade union official who had a long history of involvement in Latin American committees and operations subsidized by the CIA.[2] Could there be a more revealing commentary on the pro-war elements in the labor movement?

That same day in Detroit, Teamster International vice-president Robert Holmes voiced a different estimate of President Nixon's speech, terming it "a form of deceit which the American people will not accept." Rejecting the idea that labor should not oppose escalation of the war lest it suffer economically, Holmes insisted that only by ending the war could the problems of the nation be solved. Local 1199's Executive Council met the day after the President's speech, and adopted a resolution condemning the widening of the war. On May 5, the General Council of District 65 sent a telegram to all members of the New York State Delegation in the House of Representatives emphasizing that the President had violated Article I, Section 8 of the Constitution which declares that Congress shall have the power to declare war, and that members of Congress should file a motion of impeachment of President Nixon "so that the Constitutional process may ensue."[3] On May 6, the Philadelphia *Daily News* carried an advertisement inserted by Local 590, American Federation of State, County and Municipal Employees which urged George Meany "to call a nationwide general strike of all AFL-CIO members in protest against President Nixon's actions to continue and expand the war in Southeast Asia."

On May 6, UAW President Walter Reuther sent a telegram to the White House. It was Reuther's last public statement—he was killed in an airplane accident on the same day—and it was a sharp attack against President Nixon's war policy. Speaking for 1,800,000 members, Reuther noted that "widening the war at this point in time once again merely reinforces the bankruptcy of our policy of force and violence in Vietnam." He closed:

With the exception of a small minority, the American people, including our young people, reject violence in all

its forms as morally repugnant and counter-productive.
The problem, Mr. President, is that we cannot successfully
preach non-violence at home while we escalate mass violence abroad.

It is your responsibility to lead us out of the Southeast
Asian War—to peace at home and abroad. We must
mobilize for peace rather than for wider theaters of war in
order to turn our resources and the hearts, hands and
minds of our people to the fulfillment of America's un-
finished agenda at home.

In a statement calling for "immediate peace in Southeast Asia," the majority of the delegates to the AFL-
CIO Federation of Labor of the Greater Cleveland area
endorsed Reuther's last public utterance, as serving "in
part as a memorial for the high ideas for which he
stood. We want to see what he fought for, peace in
America, become a reality. What better memorial can
be offered than immediate peace in Southeast Asia?
May the objectives of his life be realized, and his last
public words be transformed from dream to reality."
Among the signers were Patrick J. O'Malley, president
of the Cleveland Federation of Labor; Sebastian Lupica,
executive secretary, and John Osters, president, Lake
County Federation of Labor.[4]

On May 7, the General Executive Board of the
United Electrical, Radio and Machine Workers of
America, adopted a lengthy statement pointing out that
16 months after assuming office on a pledge to end the
war, Nixon had shocked the nation by invasion of still
another country in Indochina and by renewing massive
bombing of North Vietnam. The statement labelled the
killings at Kent State "a tragic product of an Administration in Washington which has made escalation of war
abroad and repression at home its most distinguishing
characteristics." It warned that "the continuation of Administration policies will result in further deterioration
of the economy, more killings in the war, more repression at home as the Administration attempts to eliminate dissent to its harmful and dangerous policies." The
UE called upon "the labor movement to join the young
people, the educators, the clergy and other sections of
the population in pressing for an end to this war."[5]

On May 7 the 18th international convention of the American Federation of State, County and Municipal Employees, adopted a far-reaching resolution condemning the war in Southeast Asia as "the most divisive and problematical fact confronting the citizens of America." After listing five specific reasons why in the nation's interests no further blood and resources be wasted in this conflict, the international union resolved that it "opposes expansion of the Vietnam war into Cambodia," and urged "immediate and total withdrawal of all U.S. armed forces from Southeast Asia, consistent with the safety of our Armed Forces, and without regard to the willingness or ability of the Thieu government to carry on the war."[6]

This is an excellent example of the change in labor sentiment on the war, as shown by this large and growing union. At the time of the Labor Peace Assembly, Jerry Wurf, president of the international, had strongly advised the large New York City District Council 37 of his union, headed by Victor Gotbaum, not to take a position against the war. But now he opened the international convention with a ringing condemnation of the war, and the convention itself adopted what was up to that time one of the strongest stands against the war.

On May 8, in Oakland, California, the Central Labor Council of Alameda County assailed President Nixon for "crimes against our Constitution," and urged Congress to cut off funds for the Cambodian invasion "as of now." Contra Costa, Marin, San Francisco, San Mateo and Santa Clara central labor councils also spoke out, calling upon Congress to censure Nixon "for his deception, dishonesty and violation of our Constitution"; to repeal the Gulf of Tonkin resolution; and to approve the McGovern-Hatfield amendment to cut off funds for U.S. combat operations in Indochina by the end of 1970. Together these councils spoke for about 400,000 workers, but the San Francisco council made clear that the delegates acted as individuals pending a referendum among their 150,000 constituents.[7]

All of these statements by unions and labor leaders opposing the escalation of the war received scant attention in the mass media. Unless the protesting labor body took pains to insert its opposition to President Nixon's war policy as a paid advertisement, it was generally ignored. Like so many similar statements by trade unions and their leaders in the week following Nixon's speech, even Walter Reuther's last public statement, his open letter to the President opposing his policy in Indochina and his attitude toward student unrest, went unnoticed by the vast majority of the newspapers.

Not so, however, with the statements and actions of the pro-war forces in the labor movement. When the predictable announcement from Meany unconditionally supporting the invasion of Cambodia and fully endorsing Nixon's policy was made public, it received front page notice in nearly all newspapers and was relayed to millions of Americans over network TV and radio. So, too, the fact that President Nixon visited AFL-CIO headquarters to express his gratitude for this support and spent 45 minutes briefing the body on his decision to send troops into Cambodia, was a big news story. Following the meeting with the President, Meany said of Nixon's action in invading Cambodia: "In this crucial hour, he should have the full support of the American people. He certainly has ours."[8] This statement, endorsed by the AFL-CIO Executive Council with three votes against and one abstention, was promptly featured in the press and interpreted as evidence that the AFL-CIO as a whole supported the escalation of the war. To lend substance to this assessment, the press pointed to the phenomenon of the hard hats.

On Friday evening, May 9, millions of television viewers saw some 300 helmeted construction workers, armed with lead pipes and crowbars, range freely through the heart of New York's financial district, attacking student and other war protesters and those who helped the injured. They saw the mob gang up on students wearing anti-war buttons; they saw on Broadway a burly worker hit a young girl on the jaw, knocking her into the gutter; a 29-year-old lawyer knocked down and stomped by workers when he tried to help a bleeding youth, and how four men kicked at a student who was already down. They saw, too, how the police stood around passively either ignoring the brutal attacks or, in some instances, joining in the assaults.[9]

Although nothing comparable to what happened in New York occurred elsewhere, in a few cities, especially in St. Louis, the hard hats imitated the slugging tactics of the New York mob. As in New York, the hard hats did not discriminate. They roughed up anti-war women as well as anti-war men in the streets.[10]

The big hard-hat event was the pro-war rally on May 20 in New York City in support of the Nixon position on the war, organized by Peter J. Brennan, president of the 200,000-member Building and Construction Trades Council of Greater New York. The evening after the rally, President Nixon put in a call to Brennan and for more than an hour thanked him for the demonstration of support, inviting him and his associates to Washington. A week later, Brennan, several of his union colleagues, and Thomas W. Gleason of the International Longshoremen's Association went to the White House to receive in person Nixon's thanks. They, in turn, gave him a gift, and the President of the United States gleefully posed for photographers wearing a hard hat.[11]

In an interview in the *New York Times*, Brennan stated flatly that the demonstrations by the hard-hat workers on May 9 and the following days had been spontaneous. "The unions had nothing to do with it," he said. "The men acted on their own. They did it because they were fed up with violence by antiwar demonstrators, by those who spat at the American flag and desecrated it."[12] The same impression of spontaneity was given by Gleason and was a feature of television commentaries and most of the accounts in the press. But a group of enterprising reporters came up with information that gave an entirely different picture.

In a letter to the *New York Times* (May 21, 1970), Tom Draper asked: "Who is compensating the construction workers for the hours without pay they're using to march up and down Broadway, to and from City Hall, raiding Pace College and attacking students and bystanders?" His query was prompted by the fact that under their contract terms, the workers were "paid strictly and only for hours on the job, even to the extent of being docked for lateness."

The question had already been answered. It had emerged clearly from investigations by reporters that union officials and construction firms had joined in promoting and encouraging the hard-hat demonstrations, and the employers closed down their jobs and paid the hard hats for marching. A construction worker, who told a reporter for the *Wall Street Journal* that his life would be in danger if he was identified, disclosed that "Bloody Friday" was organized by union stewards with the support of some contractors, and that one contractor had offered the men cash bonuses to take part in the Wall Street head-busting. "These are people I know well," he said. "They are nice, quiet guys until Friday. But I had to drag one fellow away from attacking several women. They became storm troopers."[13] The New York *Post* revealed on May 19 that bosses let workers know that they would be paid for time taken off to attack students. "Workers . . . have freely admitted taking time from their jobs to join demonstrations or battle with students, and they have not lost pay," the *Post* wrote. The *Post* did an excellent job, too, in exposing how the rampages against the anti-war protesters and the mass pro-war union rally on May 20 was organized by joint action of the ultra-right in New York, especially the right-wing sheet, the New York *Graphic,* and union officials, and that the union leadership told its members that if they did not sign the roll call at the mass rally, they would lose their pay for the day.[14]

In July appeared the famed "Agnew memo," the document alleged to have come from the desk of the Vice President and reproduced in the first issue of *Scanlan's Monthly,* which, if authentic, revealed that the CIA was behind the hard-hard demonstrations. The memorandum, dated March 11, 1970, outlined plans for the hard-hat demonstrations supporting the Administration's Indochina war policies, which, according to the memo, were to be organized in association with representatives of the Central Intelligence Agency. The existence of this "confidential" memorandum was promptly denied by Agnew, but, authentic or not, it received scant attention in the same newspapers which had played up the "spontaneous" nature of the hard-hat demonstrations, and no paper which mentioned it even bothered to investigate the matter beyond printing Agnew's denial.[15]

In the same interview in which he declared that the hard-hat demonstrations had been "spontaneous," Brennan claimed that his mail was running 20 to 1 in favor of the actions against peace demonstrators and "praising the workers for their patriotism." But letters to the editors of New York leading papers did not confirm this estimate. While there were some who saluted "the gallant construction workers," most correspondents condemned them for aping Nazi storm troopers. The most widely-publicized letter was from Professor George Wald of Harvard, Nobel Laureate in Physiology and Medicine and peace advocate, challenging construction workers to a dialogue. Wald wrote to the *New York Times* four days after "Bloody Friday":

I want to talk to the New York construction workers. They will know what I'm saying. I grew up on the streets of Brooklyn, in a tough Irish-Italian-Polish neighborhood. I talk Brooklynese.
I march with the students, and I think that the construction workers should be marching with the students. What happens to me doesn't matter. One Nobel laureate has already been killed. That was Martin Luther King. What happens to the kids—their kids, my kids—matters very much.
So I want to talk to them. Any time, any place. How about it?[16]

Wald's invitation brought no response. But a construction worker, Charles Rivers, of Ironworkers Local 455, told a rally of City College students that the majority of the members of his local did not approve of the violence against students and were talking to workers in the trade to convey this point of view. He denied that the hard hats who went on a rampage on May 9 were symbols of Americanism. "I didn't see Americans in action. I saw black shirts and brown shirts of Hitler's Germany," he told the students. Rivers also pointed out— and this information was confirmed by a number of reporters—that police and city officials had received advance warning of the attacks from construction workers who disapproved of the "storm troopers," but had done nothing to prepare to protect the peaceful anti-war protesters.[17]

As the hard hats were being hailed in the mass media as great American patriots and the President of the United States was proudly associating himself with their crude ways of displaying their Americanism, such as beating up dissenters, the U.S. Equal Employment Opportunity Commission was reporting "no progress" in the recruitment of minorities by construction unions. The EEOC found that blacks made up only 7.4 per cent of the 1.1 million members of construction union locals filing reports for 1968. The percentage of blacks in individual trades ranged from 29.2 per cent in the Laborers Union to zero in the Asbestos Workers. Puerto Rican union members and others with Spanish surnames accounted for 4.4 per cent of those surveyed. Their share varied from the Plasterers' 12.1 per cent to the Asbestos Workers' 1.1 per cent. Though the 1968 tabulation covered only one-third of the nation's 3.5 million construction union members, the EEOC report stated that it was "generally representative" of the racial makeup of the building trades. The EEOC officials emphasized *"that 75% of the Negroes in the building trades belong to the Laborers Union whose pay scales rank among the lowest."*[18]

Statistics for the area over which the great patriot Brennan reigned supreme are also revealing. The Federal Equal Opportunity Commission revealed in 1969 that in the New York metropolitan area 0.3 per cent of the union plumbers, 1.4 per cent of the bricklayers, 6.6 per cent of carpenters, and 2.7 per cent of marble polishers are black. This contrasted with the non-building trades unions where 17.9 per cent of the workers are black—still an inadequate minority representation but far ahead of the construction unions.[19]

In March 1970, under mounting pressure, Brennan finally presented a plan which was to integrate blacks and Puerto Rican workers into the building trades unions. The National Association for the Advancement of Colored People promptly labelled the plan a "hoax," and a "subterfuge," pointing out that it provided "no assurances of any kind whatsoever" that the skilled black workers enlisted in the program at $80 a week would become "union plumbers, electricians, pipefitters, and so on, when this is all over."[20] It was a correct evaluation. In St. Louis, for example, the seat of another hard-hat, pro-war demonstration by the construction workers, seven of the 18 unions, accounting for just over half of the city's 45,000 building trades membership, had committed themselves to hiring blacks. The plan was held up until $524,500 in federal training funds came through in July 1970. Within a week, 25 blacks were being trained, but not in highly paid unions like the electricians, plumbers and steam fitters.[21]

Little wonder that Mark Lerner, a hard hat himself, but one who could not swallow the talk of "patriotism" in the pro-war, hard-hat demonstrations, wrote, in a letter published in the *St. Louis Post-Dispatch* on June 8, 1970:

I worked as a construction worker for 30 years. I worked out of several different locals in several different states; also Alaska and South America, and I wore a hard hat and I was also hard-headed—hard-headed because as the highest paid workers in America we looked down on the rest of Americans and even had the gall to call them peasants.

We were and still are only interested in our own interests. We have never been known to help any union to raise their living standard other than another construction union. We condone business agents, financial secretaries and presidents who are as crooked as they come.

In almost every construction craft in the United States the rank and file members have nothing to say as to who are their national officers. It goes without saying that once a national officer is elected he stays there until he dies. In all my years as a construction worker I was never a member of a local that had one black man in it. What gall they have to wear an American flag decal on their hard hats.

Small wonder, too, that the few black and Spanish-speaking workers in the building trades took little part in the hard-hat demonstrations. (At the pro-war union rally on May 20, black workers present frankly told reporters that the only reason they were there was that they would lose their pay for the day if they stayed away.[22]) One black carpenter, a World War II veteran, denounced his parading brethren as "make-believe patriots and cowards." The New York chapter of the National Afro-American Labor Council issued a statement informing the hard-hat bullies to "walk softly and keep their mouths shut" at construction sites in New York's black neighborhood. These leading black trade unionists of New York characterized the assaults on peace demonstrators as "deeds of a racist union which has now turned to repressive violence against students and blacks."[23]

On July 25 members of the Committee of the Planning Professions to End the War in Vietnam arrived in Washington to lobby for the McGovern-Hatfield Amendment. The group was only one of many which descended upon the nation's capital during the weeks following the extension of the war into Cambodia. But the fact that it was made up of architects, engineers, and builders—in short, representatives of an industry that had become the symbol of the hard hats—aroused more than usual interest. Addressing the Committee, Republican Senator Charles E. Goodell of New York, a vigorous opponent of the war, told them: "I think it's very important we communicate with the so-called hard hats . . . they suffer just as much or more from the war as others do."[24] This viewpoint was becoming more and more a feature of discussions of the "hard hat syndrome." It was a mistake, went the argument, to view the hard hats as "born fascists" and "natural enemies" of the peace movement. Some insisted that no real progress could be made toward stopping the war unless these workers were recruited for the cause. While few condoned the brutal attacks on those with whom the hard hats disagreed, they insisted that it was necessary to understand that much of it stemmed from legitimate if misunderstood gripes. The hard hats, went the discussion, were worried and frightened men, but they did not understand the real reason for their concerns. True, their paychecks were fatter, yet their money bought less; they had worked hard to get where they were, yet they saw their jobs threatened by invasion of blacks and Puerto Ricans; they had finally reached the point where they could enjoy a decent home, and they were scared that their property values would vanish if blacks and Puerto Ricans moved into the neighborhood. Many were children of the depression and had had no chance to get a college education, yet they saw draft-deferred college students, mostly from the affluent middle or upper class, wasting their time in demonstrations and riots. They had fought for their country in World War II and the Korean War and their sons and relatives were fighting and dying in Vietnam, and they were told it was all for nothing but advancing the interests of American imperialism. They had been taught in school and church to venerate the flag, yet they saw youthful demonstrators spitting at and burning it. In short, the world they believed in was disintegrating before their eyes, and unable to understand the complex reasons for it and failing to relate their economic problems to the war, they hit out with brute force at those they had been told were really responsible for their problems.

Some even charged that the beating up of student war protesters was the inevitable result of years of indifference on the part of the anti-war movement, largely academic in composition, "toward people who work with their hands for a living and its willingness not only to ignore them, but to go even further and alienate them completely." Jimmy Breslin, who was one of those who advanced this argument, added that "the beatings handed out by construction workers should have started a process of rearranging a few attitudes."[25]

The problem was how to link the deep-seated concerns of these workers to the war issue. Some in the peace movement answered that all this psychoanalysis of

the hard hats was all very well, but how does one get to
them with a peace message without risking being sent to
the hospital? A few peace workers, however, tried. During the work stoppage for peace conducted by several
thousand members of the book publishing and film industries, June 17, several young girls on the editorial
staffs of publishers talked to groups of construction
workers about the war, inflation, and taxes, and distributed literature among them on how to get out of Vietnam. While they reported they had not been able to
convince many, they at least came away intact.[26] In
Chicago a group of anti-war building trades workers reported greater success. They got out a leaflet entitled
"Who are the Patriots?" and distributed copies in mid-
June at 15 construction sites in and near the Loop. The
leaflet stressed that "hard hats are not necessarily hard
heads incapable of logic or the lessons of recent history." It asked, "What are the issues? . . . Patriotism?
. . . Students?" And it answered:

The real issues are:
The basic concept of the war in Vietnam is wrong and im-
moral.
Poverty in this land of opulence is inhuman and unneces-
sary.
This country is sick with racism.

The leaflet concluded with the statement that no
problems facing the workers could really be solved until
the war was ended, and urged the construction workers
to "defend and advance the rights of black and minority
workers in the interest of strengthening and broaden-
ing the trade union movement." A reporter who accompanied the leaflet distributors wrote that "at least 90 per
cent of the men we talked to were against the war and
almost all thought that beating up the students was just
plain stupid. A surprising number were convinced that
the 'hard hats' had been paid to march and attack the
students. Most workers we talked with blamed Nixon
and his war policy for unemployment and strikes."[27]

Readers of the San Francisco *Chronicle* of June 10
learned something new about the hard hats. Hodcarrier
Walter Stack, a member of his local union's executive

board, was shown in the paper seated on his bicycle with a sign around his neck that read, "Hard Hats—Not All Stormtroopers." He told the *Chronicle* that he had been disturbed by the image the public had formed of construction workers after the hard hats went on a rampage in New York and St. Louis, and that he had decided to get on his bicycle with his sign and ride up Market Street past the Bay Area Transport Tunnel site. Construction workers who saw him were very friendly, he reported, and many gave him the V-sign as he rode by. Stack also told the *Chronicle* that the next day when he returned to work, many of his fellow construction workers, who had seen his picture in the paper, thanked him for expressing their feelings. Most construction workers, Stack insisted, were against the war, and he pointed out that eight of the nine Bay Area Labor councils had passed anti-war resolutions calling for the censure of President Nixon.

All this did not mean that there were no hard hats who were vehement in support of the war and would, given the opportunity, repeat their attacks on anti-war protesters. But it is also clear that not all hard hats were pro-war, that many who demonstrated in favor of it did so because they were compelled to, and that the vast majority of the hard hats were not beyond reach by the peace movement.

6

LABOR-STUDENT ALLIANCES

"HARD HATS OR NOT, AMERICAN LABOR IS SPEAKING OUT AGAINST THE WAR." THIS WAS THE TITLE OF an article by Henry Foner, president of the Joint Board Fur, Leather and Machine Workers, published in its official journal *Tempo,* July 1970. While the demonstrations of the hard hats had been interpreted by the mass media as evidence that organized labor was solidly in the pro-war camp, a viewpoint reinforced by the praise lavished on the leaders of the construction workers and the longshoremen by President Nixon, labor leaders, most of them representing unions far larger than the Building Trades Council and the ILA, were continuing to condemn the extension of the war into Cambodia. Trade union officials who had supported Meany's war policy, more often with silence than with active endorsement, now agreed that this was just too much, and that it was time to get out.

On the Saturday following "Bloody Friday," 120,000 war protesters gathered at a hastily convened demonstration on the Ellipse near the White House. Among them were delegations of trade unionists from various Eastern cities as well as contingents from the Washington Labor Peace Committee and even a federal workers' peace unit. David Livingston of District 65 publicly branded the hard hats who attacked the peace demonstrators as "hoodlums" and "stormtroopers," and went on "to offer the apologies of the decent people in the labor movement for the stormtrooper activities of some construction workers in New York yesterday. They do not represent labor. The hoodlums of yesterday are doing George Meany's work, and we ought to call him for the fink he is." He urged the crowd, made up largely of students, not to be misled by Meany's claim that labor supported the war, pointing out that the two largest unions in the world, the United Auto Workers and the Teamsters, had supported the October 15 and November 15 mobilizations.[1] The *New York Times* of May 13, 1970 reported that leaders of more than a dozen New York City unions condemned the construction workers attack on war protesters.

The advance copy of the editorial in the June-July issue of *The Butcher Workman,* official organ of the Amalgamated Meat Cutters and Butcher Workmen, was released to the press early in May. Entitled "War and the AFL-CIO," it rejected Meany's war stand. Noting that Senator Fulbright had had "the courage to state that the AFL-CIO has become part of the military establishment," it conceded that this "serious charge" was "to a great extent . . . true." Pointing out further that universities throughout the country, both students and administrators, practically every church denomination in the country, fraternal orders and groups, even bankers had joined with millions of peace demonstrators in advocating "the stopping of this human slaughter," the editorial asked: "Is everybody out of step except the AFL-CIO?" Its answer was clear: "The AFL-CIO is not infallible, and many of us feel strongly that it is out of step with the thinking of the 13,000,000 members it represents."[2]

On May 13, representatives of New York's organized hospital workers, the Executive Council of Local 1199, met and adopted a resolution condemning the widened war, repudiating the pro-war policies of Meany and the AFL-CIO Executive Council, and denouncing the "patriotism" of "ruffians [who] disgrace the name of labor." The resolution welcomed into the ranks of the anti-war movement "the thousands of people of all ages who now have been moved to do something as a result of the Cambodian outrage and its consequence." It closed: "We say: End the War. Stop the Killing!"[3]

On May 9, a hard-hitting message to President Nixon, calling for an end to the war now, signed by 451 trade union leaders, was published as a full page advertisement in both the San Francisco *Chronicle* and *The Examiner*. Titled, "We've had it!" the ad informed President Nixon:

You have created a credibility gap of incredible proportions.

You have pledged to the American people that we will be out of Cambodia by June 30.

In the light of this record, all we can say is—we don't believe you!

The economy of our country is steadily being eroded; your promises to stabilize the economy and control inflation have become meaningless. Our paychecks buy less for our families; our standard of living has been assaulted. We are suffering increased inflation and unemployment.

Now Cambodia! What next?

There must be an end to these military adventures.

We want a cease-fire—Now!

We want out of Cambodia—Now!

We want out of Vietnam—Now!

We've had it!.

Most important, this nation of ours must turn from war to peace. Any other course leads to disaster.

The advertisement made news not only on the West Coast but throughout the nation as newspapers which had ignored similar labor protests carried stories from San Francisco describing the message to President Nixon as an important development in the labor movement. The *New York Times* correspondent described it as "the shattering of labor union support in this area for President Nixon's Indochina policies." He noted that "while the sentiments expressed in the advertisement are not new, the signatures to such a document of the names of many leaders of conservative unions constitutes a departure from national labor policy."[4]

Among the signers whose names came as a surprise were:

A. Figone, executive secretary, San Francisco District Council of Carpenters; Daniel Del Carlo, chairman, San Francisco Building Trades Council; Charles Brown, executive board member, Ironworkers Local 790; G. P. Campbell, assistant business manager, Boilermakers; Samuel C. Churchwell, business representative, Local 224,

Plasterers; Einar Mohn, second national vice president, Teamsters, and head of Western Conference of Teamsters; Joseph Diviny, first national vice president, Teamsters; Larry Vail, secretary, State Retail Clerks' Union; Richard Grouix, executive secretary, Alameda County Labor Council.

Actually, as we have seen, several had already placed themselves on record against the war, but this had never attracted the attention achieved by the advertisements in both San Francisco papers. One of the signers had been forced to suffer long imprisonment because of his militancy in the cause of labor and peace on the eve of World War I. He was Warren K. Billings who had been sentenced to life imprisonment with Tom Mooney on the charge of having set off a bomb during the San Francisco Preparedness Day parade of 1915, a charge later proved false. After he was pardoned and released from prison, Billings had returned to the labor movement and was elected to the executive board of a Watchmakers local.

While precedent was being broken on the West Coast three thousand miles away in New York an event unprecedented in labor history was also occurring. For the first time since the anti-war movement was launched, trade unions and students met to plan a joint end-the-war rally at New York's City Hall on May 21. Two steering committees were set up: one representing the labor organizations—AFL-CIO, ALA and independent unions—and the other, college students from universities and colleges in the New York metropolitan area. Coordinator for the labor organizations was Moe Foner, executive secretary of Local 1199, while Ed Strickland, a New York University graduate student, was coordinator for the student organizations.

Labor-student unity was achieved, after considerable negotiating, on the basis of a three-point program which was to become the demands of the rally: "End the war in Vietnam and Cambodia *Now;* Protest the killings at Kent State, Augusta and Jackson; Stop the Repression Against Dissent and Protest." New Yorkers were soon treated to the unusual sight of students and workers separately and jointly distributing leaflets at busy street corners announcing a Labor-Student Rally to Stop the War, to be held at City Hall Park, Thursday, May 21, 12 Noon to 2 p.m., sponsored by the Labor-Student Coalition for Peace. The leaflet listed as unions participating in the coalition:

Amalgamated Clothing Workers; Drug and Hospital; Electrical; Bakery and Confectionary; Hotel and Restaurant; Furniture; State, County and Municipal; Jewelry; Store Workers; Distributive; Book and Magazine Guild; Motion Picture Operators, and Fur and Leather Workers.

Schools participating were: Brooklyn College, CCNY, Columbia University, Cooper Union, Lehman, Yeshiva, Marymount, Manhattan, New York University, New School, Queens College, Hunter, NYU Law School, Mills College of Education, Princeton University.

In all 15 trade unions and 15 campuses in the metropolitan area were included in the first Labor-Student Coalition for Peace in American history.

The executive board of Local 1707 of the State, County and Municipal Workers, an AFL-CIO affiliate, voted to call for a one-day stoppage May 21 to support the labor-student peace rally. The Social Service Employees Union, whose members were in private social agencies, voted to back the demonstration.[5] When rumors spread throughout the city that a group of hard hats were preparing to turn the rally into a "Bloody Thursday," rank-and-file unionists and students organized into security guards.

On May 21 at noon City Hall Park was jammed with workers and students, many carrying signs reading, "Meany Doesn't Speak For Me," "Peace Now," Avenge Kent State and Jackson State," "Avenge Augusta." Ossie Davis, the distinguished black actor, writer and director, opened the rally by saying he came in the name of "a pantheon of heroes—Dr. Du Bois, Dr. King, Malcolm X, and Paul Robeson." Ed Strickland, speaking for the students, declared: "Our honor can never be won by killing. Our honor can be won by using this nation's resources for its people. The frightening escalation of the President's power leaves us at the mercy of a man

Labor says: "END THE WAR!"

LABOR COMMITTEE
of the DETROIT COALITION
to END THE WAR NOW
5705 Woodward · Detroit 48202
Phone: 873-4322

LABOR VOICE for PEACE

Weekly Newsletter of
MADISON LABOR AGAINST THE WAR

ATTEND THE

LABOR-STUDENT RALLY

TO

- END THE WAR IN VIETNAM AND CAMBODIA NOW!
- PROTEST THE KILLINGS AT KENT STATE, AUGUSTA AND JACKSON STATE.
- STOP THE REPRESSION AGAINST DISSENT AND PROTEST.

CITY HALL PARK
THURSDAY, MAY 21, 12 NOON TO 2 P.M.

Call to a

NATIONAL RANK·AND·FILE ACTION CONFERENCE

SATURDAY-SUNDAY, JUNE 27-28, 1970
PACKINGHOUSE LABOR AND COMMUNITY CENTER
4859 S. WABASH AVENUE
CHICAGO, ILLINOIS

A sampling of labor peace activities from Madison, Wisc., Chicago, New York and Detroit.

who called us bums and bomb throwers." William By-water, District 3, International Union of Electrical Workers, asked: "Will those labor leaders who say they support our boys in Vietnam give jobs to black vets when they come back? That's the true test of patriotism." Doris Turner, executive vice president of Local 1199, promised: "We will work for the defeat of any candidate—from dogcatcher to president—who does not stand squarely and unequivocally against the war."[6]

How many attended the labor-student rally is difficult to determine accurately. The Steering Committee claimed 50,000 while the press mainly emphasized that the anti-war demonstration fell far short of the previous day's pro-war rally. Most of the New York papers ignored nearly all of what took place at the demonstration at City Hall, devoting their headlines and news accounts to the fact that nine were injured by the police after militant students had insisted on marching uptown instead of dispersing after the rally. The police, chafing at the restraints that had been imposed upon their conduct after "Bloody Friday," had a chance to show their dislike of anti-war protesters since the students did not have a permit for the parade. "With nightsticks extended," wrote the reporter for the *New York Times,* "they charged into the ranks of marchers, sending youths sprawling and putting the rest to panicky flight."[7]

The New York labor-student rally was not the only example of labor-student cooperation during the national crisis following the extension of the war into Cambodia. An anti-war advertisement, published at the University of California, was signed jointly by students, teachers and union members, including members of some building trades unions. In Chicago labor and students joined in a mass march on May 23 to protest the killing of students at Kent State and Jackson State and of black people in Augusta, and to express opposition to the war in Southeast Asia. Labor and students were also together on the March Against Repression through the state of Georgia, called by the Southern Christian Leadership Conference, to protest the slaying of Blacks in

Augusta and Jackson, and demand immediate withdrawal of U.S. forces from Indochina. As his first act after he was named President of the UAW to replace the late Walter Reuther, Leonard Woodcock flew to Atlanta to join the marchers.[8]

Throughout the remainder of May, important sections of the labor movement continued to take a strong stand against the war. It is impossible fully to report all the actions taken so extensive were they. Numerous locals, some national unions, city and state councils, district and regional bodies, AFL-CIO and ALA affiliates and independent unions, voiced their indignation at the escalation of the war and called for an end to the carnage. The St. Paul *Union Advocate* reported that the Trades and Labor Council of that Minnesota city had taken a firm stand against the war after a heated discussion.[9]

In an editorial *Labor,* the national journal of 14 railroads and airline unions, urged the end of "the festering Vietnam war because the longer the war drags on, the greater will be the divisiveness at home. America should get out of Cambodia. U.S. troops should be withdrawn from Vietnam on an expedited timetable."[10]

More and more unions, however, no longer qualified their demand for withdrawal of U.S. troops from Indochina with an "expedited timetable" clause, but asked for an end to the war now. And in assailing the use of force against dissent, they now included Augusta and Jackson State as well as Kent State in their condemnation. In its first major policy statement following the death of Walter Reuther, the United Auto Workers called for an end to the use of armed forces against Americans, black and white, dissenting from government policies. "The terrible shame of violence by government has cast a grim and ominous shadow across our nation in recent weeks. It is a shadow that has dimmed the right of democratic rule in Kent, Ohio, in Jackson, Mississippi, and in Augusta, Ga."[11]

This statement was released to the nation from Detroit by the UAW International Executive Board on May 25. That same day the 27th biennial convention of the Amalgamated Clothing Workers of America opened in Atlantic City. In his keynote address before 1,500 delegates, General President Jacob S. Potofsky, head of the 417,000-member union and a member of the AFL-CIO Executive Council, publicly broke with the AFL-CIO leadership and condemned the Vietnam and Cambodian war policies of the Nixon Administration. For close to an hour he examined in detail every aspect of the war in Vietnam, particularly the disastrous effects it was having on the nation. He noted that it had greatly damaged "the spirit of America. . . . It has brought back some of the evils of McCarthyism. . . . Today, we have tapped wires, political snooping, secret informers—all of them the marks not of a democracy but of a police state. Our Bill of Rights is in danger of erosion. Until we have peace, our very democratic processes are threatened." One of the greatest tragedies arising from the war, Potofsky insisted, was what had happened to the youth of America, "so many of whom have lost much of their faith in our leadership and in our democratic system. Students are not saints, but neither are they bums or rotten apples."

The Amalgamated's President concluded his lengthy analysis of the effects of the war with a discussion of unemployment and inflation, and pointed out that both were inextricably related to the continuation of the war and could not be halted effectively until peace was achieved in Southeast Asia.[12]

Most newspapers agreed that Potofsky's condemnation of the war policy of the Nixon Administration, though late in coming, represented a significant break in the top AFL-CIO leadership. "His position," noted the *New York Times,* "has additional significance because he is a senior member of the AFL-CIO Executive Council, which has consistently supported United States policy in Southeast Asia."[13]

The delegates to the Amalgamated convention put the giant clothing union on record against the war, adopting a resolution which termed the invasion of Cambodia a "tragic mistake from every point of view." They called for withdrawal of all combat troops in Indochina by the end of 1970, and complete withdrawal of all American military presence there by June 1971.[14]

While national, state and local unions were passing resolutions against the war, peace committees or caucuses were being organized in unions in a number of cities. Work stoppages occurred as an expression of opposition to the war. On May 15, during the tribute to Walter Reuther, a work stoppage took place at the Chicago Ford Assembly plant. After the scheduled three-minute memorial was over, some 2,000 workers continued the stoppage for the rest of the day as a tribute to the late labor leader's opposition to continuation of the war and to repression at home. (In Detroit, a similar stoppage occurred at about 20 plants.)[15]

During June and July the anti-war protests of organized labor continued. Despite what Charles Boyle, president of the International Chemical Workers, called "tremendous pressure" from the White House "and other sources," in mid-June came the news that labor leaders representing 13 international unions, with millions of members, had formed the National Labor Committee to End the War in Indochina. Co-chairmen were Boyle of the International Chemical Workers and Charles Hayes, vice president of the Amalgamated Meat Cutters, with Mazey of the United Auto Workers as coordinator. The initial project of the group was to rally union support for the Cooper-Church Amendment A. 609, "The Amendment to End the War" by cutting off funds for U.S. combat operations in Indochina. But the larger objective was to combat the image of labor in the mass media. "We are particularly concerned about the image given to organized labor by the hard hats," Hayes told reporters. "The time has come for patriotic Americans to show that we can have peace." Boyle noted that President Nixon in his so-called anti-inflation campaign had said nothing about profits and dividends but had focused instead on ways to "make the workers pay" for continuing the war while seemingly fighting inflation. Mazey added that "a nation wasting $30 billion a year for the war could better use the money for housing, education and health care."[16]

In June, two other international unions broke with their past silence on the war. The RWDSU convention, where Local 1199's delegation played a leading role, passed a resolution in favor of "early and orderly withdrawal of all U.S. armed forces from Indochina," and the American Newspaper Guild approved one calling "for immediate withdrawal of all United States armed forces from Southeast Asia."[17]

On June 16 Leonard Woodcock testified· before the Joint Economic Committee of Congress, engaged in holding hearings on the nation's priorities. The UAW president presented a 91-page manifesto to the Committee touching on every phase of the crisis facing the United States. He condemned as "phony" President Nixon's claim that high wages are the cause of inflation, and told the Committee that ending the Vietnam war was the real cure for soaring unemployment, huge taxes, astronomical prices, and the collapse of the cities.[18]

During the last weekend of June, the National Rank and File Action Conference (or National Labor Action Conference) was held in Chicago. The 556 delegates, 288 observers and 31 visitors came from 25 states and the District of Columbia, from about 30 different occupational groups. Twenty-six were local union officers; 157 came from rank-and-file caucuses, including black caucuses. Unorganized groups were present as were unemployed, students and groups of striking workers.

For two days the delegates conducted deliberations in a crowded convention hall, in panel discussions on issues, in caucuses of state delegations, occupational and union groups. There were five major areas of concern: (1) how to defend trade union and rank-and-file rights; (2) how to combat racism and advance the rights of black and minority group workers; (3) how to advance the rights of women workers; (4) how to advance the rights of working youth; (5) how to advance peace and labor political action. Problems created by the war, by racism, by increased exploitation and the government's repressive policies were central to all discussions. The building trades caucus, speaking as "hard hats," sent out a communication to the trades leadership calling on them to dissociate themselves from the legislation proposed by the Nixon Administration that would deny rank-and-file workers the right to vote on contract ratification. It called on building trades councils all over the nation to demand utilization of war funds for construction of houses and schools, instead of for killing people. The caucus also urged trades leaders to wipe out the image of the building trades as a stronghold of racism.

Not all were in agreement at the conference on all issues. But there was complete unanimity on the significance of intensified effort to end the war. Speaker after speaker attacked the war in Indochina as a major cause of repression and recession. Charles Hayes, international vice president of the Amalgamated Meat Cutters, challenged Meany's claim that the labor movement supported President Nixon's foreign policy and most specifically, the Cambodian invasion. He declared that the rising opposition of organized labor to the war proved how wrong were those who "think the labor movement is hopeless," and urged that it was necessary to "work within it rather than turn one's back on it." He told the conference that "people like you are going to steer the trade unions along a different course [than that of Meany] because many in the labor movement have long been concerned about the direction it has taken and this conference is taking the right course." He closed on a prophetic note: "You are going to change the course of the labor movement."

With this as its purpose the delegates launched the National Coordinating Committee for Trade Union Action and Democracy with a 115-member coordinating body.[19] It is too early as of this writing to gauge the effectiveness of this new anti-war body, especially among the workers. Local and regional Labor Action Committees, affiliated with the National Coordinating Committee, have already come into existence and begun to make their presence felt. These Committees are holding meetings and conferences to widen support for the objectives of the rank-and-file movement: "Defeat racism;

unite black and white workers; defend the membership's right to strike; and put labor on record against the war in Indochina."[20]

It is likely that rank-and-file movements now under way will bring labor closer to the position of the students. In any event, it is of importance not to ignore the fact that one result of labor's increasing involvement in the anti-war movement has been the growing realization on the part of the leaders of the anti-war unions of a need to achieve closer relations with the students. Precisely at the time that George Meany, in his interview with labor reporters late in August, was lashing out at "hippies, marijuana smoking and lax morals," and indicating a total unwillingness to achieve any contact "with the present generation of young people," representatives of over 500 student governments across the nation were meeting with trade unionists at the 23rd National Student Congress in St. Paul. While Meany was discoursing at length on how the members of the AFL-CIO "have become middle class," and hence had no interest in radical change in American society, United Auto Workers' President Leonard Woodcock was telling the students that "the auto worker is not a part of the affluent middle class." While Meany was declaring that strikes were outmoded today, Woodcock was informing the students that their assistance would be welcomed if a long "strike in the old fashioned way" was the outcome of a breakdown in current negotiations with the Big Three auto makers and the agricultural implements industry. Although he warned that it would be fatal if a group of students moved in and told the workers, "We're going to show you how to do things," he stressed that real cooperation between the two groups could be achieved in the event of a strike and would do much to eliminate any existing hostility.

The discussions between the unionists and the students at the NSA convention revealed that basic differences in outlook persisted. Students still believe that even the anti-war unionists had been remiss in not having called for their members to strike during the invasion of Cambodia, while the union leaders made it clear that they did not have the power to undertake such a course of action. But the very fact that these differences were being aired and other issues discussed by students and trade unionists marked an important turning-point in the history of both movements.[21]

Another sign of this new trend was the letter published in the Minneapolis *Tribune* of June 14, signed by David Roe, president of the Minnesota AFL-CIO and three officials of the Minneapolis Central Labor Union, appealing for a "working relationship with students and faculty against the war and other social evils in our society," and urging that they work together and "with other interested segments of society to plan a course of action mutually beneficial to the basic interests of these groups and to the community." The unionists pointed out that students, workers and other members of the community were faced with the same problems, among them "unemployment, inflation, threats of repression, an unpopular war and administrations hostile and unresponsive at various levels of government." They proposed that students and labor begin a dialogue on how to solve these problems.

Still another sign of the new trend was the full-page labor-student advertisement in the Cleveland *Plain Dealer* of June 2, 1970 condemning the war in Indochina. The statement, signed by 42 Cleveland labor leaders and 21 area educators and student leaders, quoted Walter Reuther's last public statement in which the late head of the UAW called the Nixon invasion of Cambodia a "tragedy" which "reinforces the bankruptcy of our policy of force and violence in Vietnam." The labor signers represented the UAW, Carpenters, Painters, Meatcutters, Steelworkers, Teamsters and Printers, and included the president and executive secretary of the Cleveland AFL-CIO and four members of the Executive Board. What is significant, too, is that signatures and contributions for the ad were gathered by the Case Western Reserve University Labor Action Committee, a student group which was organized for the purpose of uniting labor, students and educators in anti-war activities.

Then there is the significant fact that at a press conference in Detroit, late in May, Gus Scholle, AFL-CIO president, and Grady Glenn, Ford Local 600 president, told newsmen they were working for united action by the student peace movement and organized labor. Students were right, Scholle said, "in protesting Nixon's slash of $1½ billion for aid to education while spending $120 billion for war." Glenn, a Vietnam war veteran, added that the billions Scholle spoke about "being spent for this racist war and armaments could rebuild the ghettos that scar our land." Asked by a reporter if it were true that union men and women "are for the war because it means big take-home money for them," Scholle replied:

First let me say, there are over 5 million jobless in America. So war does not bring prosperity to the workers.

Secondly, war inflation is eating up the wages and increases faster than the workers can bring it home.

Third, whose sons are being killed and wounded in these wars? It's workers' sons.

Fourth, who pays the most for taxes? Almost 50 per cent of a worker's income goes for taxes. And workers are not for war, were never for war.

This is one reason I am here on this podium to extend the hand to students of cooperation and dialogue, so we get to understand one another and march down the road together for peace and an end to this war.[22]

Indicative of the same trend, was the announcement, September 15, 1970, in Washington, of a formal labor-student alliance, supplemented by professors, black leaders and clergy, to elect anti-war Congressmen in the fall elections. The newly-formed "National Coalition for a Responsible Congress" has on its board Leonard Woodcock, UAW president, Jerry Wurf, president of the American Federation of State, County and Municipal Employees, and officials of Amalgamated Meat Cutters and Amalgamated Clothing Workers. Former Attorney General Ramsey Clark is chairman of the group, and the steering committee includes a number of outstanding church, civil rights and peace leaders, as well as professors and students.[23] Whatever may have been accomplished in the November 1970 elections by the new group, the existence of the Coalition is further evidence that a labor-student alliance has gone beyond the talking stage.

The same may be said of an alliance between sections of the trade unions and the liberal academic community. In October 1970, at the initiative of Professor George Wald, the Nobel Prize laureate in biology and outspoken critic of the Vietnam War, union officials, teachers and students met at Harvard University. The meeting ended with the formation of a national committee of union, student and faculty members charged with the task of establishing local organizations in metropolitan centers around the country. Woodcock and Potofsky are the union representatives on the committee. The organization will seek to change the foreign and economic policies of the Nixon Administration, and a speedy end to the war in Indochina is one of its chief objectives.

As we close this account of labor's opposition to the war in Indochina the war still continues. The great protests of the spring of 1970, in which the anti-war unions were an integral part, did compel Nixon to pledge "withdrawal" of American troops from Cambodia. However, Nixon continues to send American planes and helicopters as part of U.S. military assistance to the Lon Nol government or, as Prince Norodom Sihanouk wrote in *The Nation* of September 14, 1970, "the Fascist and bloody dictatorship of the Lon Nol junta." The Hatfield-McGovern "end the war amendment" has gone down to defeat in the Senate even after its sponsors amended it to lengthen the time American troops would remain in Indochina. Still it is possible to obtain some comfort from the fact that 39 Senate votes were cast against President Nixon's war policy in the 55–39 vote on Hatfield-McGovern. Never before in wartime has a President met with such a rebuff.

George Meany still continues to give President Nixon assurances of his support for his goal of military victory in Southeast Asia. In a group interview with six labor reporters in Washington during the last week of August, Meany declared that the AFL-CIO was in "basic agreement" with Nixon's Vietnam policies and "completely opposed to the idea of bugging out."[24] Such support, *Time* reported, along with "parades of hard hats backing Administration policy in Southeast Asia," has nullified whatever peace sentiment exists in organized labor and "warmed the President personally."[25]

But even as Meany spoke and *Time* dismissed the anti-war trade unions, international unions, local, district and regional labor bodies, and labor leaders in increasing numbers were continuing to vote and speak against the war, and rank-and-file movements were springing up around the country to organize even more effectively working class opposition to the war. Inflation, rising unemployment* and soaring taxes continue to hit labor and to give ever-increasing weight to the arguments of the anti-war forces in organized labor. In prominent places throughout Detroit there are large posters placed by the United Auto Workers reading, "Fight Inflation—End the War Now!"

Late in November 1970, President Nixon once again escalated the war by bombing North Vietnam. A wave of indignation swept through labor's ranks, but as Robert Holmes, international vice president of the Teamsters observed: "Just being upset about this is not enough. . . . Let us make Congress stop the Pentagon." Labor-student-academic coalitions are being organized in a number of cities to achieve this objective.

As the Nixon Administration expanded the war into Cambodia and Laos, the International Executive Board of the United Auto Workers, meeting on January 30, 1971, vigorously condemned the deeper involvement in Indochina. "This Administration, which came to power on the promise to disengage from war in South Vietnam, is clearly not keeping its pledge," the Board declared. Stressing the violation of its mandate to the people, the statement continued: "We thus unreservedly condemn the use of any American troops in Cambodia in the air,

* "4.6 Million Unemployed; Rate Highest in 7½ Years," read a headline in the *New York Times,* December 5, 1970. A month later (January 9, 1971), the headline in the *Times* read: "Jobless Rate up to 6% in Nation; Highest Since '61."

on the ground or by any other means." The Administration's intent to win the war was based on a "fallacy" which should have become clear in the years since the United States became involved in Indochina. "Let us now commit ourselves to a speedy end to the war and the restoration of peaceful conditions in Indochina," the UAW Board urged.

The evidence of rising opposition in labor's ranks to the war is clear. In themselves, the resolutions, speeches and activities of the anti-war trade unions and rank-and-file movements may not result in bringing about an immediate change in the pro-war policies of the AFL-CIO leadership nor in ending the immoral and unjust war. But already the peace movement has acquired the backing of an important and ever-increasing section of the American labor movement which has committed itself "to continue our efforts together with all other forces in the trade union movement and elsewhere, to guarantee that the voice of American labor is heard loud and clear for PEACE NOW!"[26]

7

CONCLUSION

WHEN I MENTIONED LABOR OPPOSITION TO THE WAR IN
SOUTHEAST ASIA DURING A LECTURE TOUR OF A NUM-
ber of universities and colleges in March 1970, my
statement produced a reaction of disbelief or ridicule
from students and faculty alike. One student at a West
Coast university confronted me with the following sen-
tence from an article published in *Monthly Review* of
May 1966: "It is not the organized white workers of the
United States who have demonstrated against the brutal
acts of American imperialism in Vietnam but students,
intellectuals, and professional people." He then added
that what was true in 1966 was just as true in 1970. The
audience applauded him vigorously. In general the viewpoint of most students was that the working class in this
country was too hopelessly backward and reactionary
and the labor leadership too intimately linked to the
power structure to expect a record of labor opposition
to the war in Indochina.

It is not too difficult to understand the disenchantment of young Americans with the labor movement. For
one thing, they know little of the militant traditions of
the American working class. Even unfamiliar to most
are events as recent as the dramatic struggles of the
1930's when workers fought the world's most powerful
corporations for the basic right to be "treated as human
beings and not as part of the machinery," as one worker
put it in the greatest of all the struggles of this period—
the 1937 battle in Flint, Michigan between the General
Motors Corporation and the sit-down strikers representing the United Auto Workers. How, then, could they
know what it took for these workers to alter the pattern
of industrial feudalism that characterized most American corporations in the years before the CIO launched

the organization of the mass production industries and what it required in sacrifice to achieve this organization?

But this is not the labor movement with which the youth of America are familiar. They know, instead, a labor movement that by and large has lost its fervor for larger social issues and opts instead only for a larger slice of "the great American pie"; a movement that is either laggard or silent on such issues as poverty, minority rights, and peace. They have seen how some unions have generously supported protest demonstrations and legislation to improve the lot of blacks while the labor movement by and large still resisted the entrance of blacks into their ranks, a movement whose leadership was nearly lily-white. More than that, they have been made well aware through the press that the AFL-CIO leadership, without real opposition from the affiliated unions, had become the active supporter at home and abroad of America's cold-war diplomacy, and that the AFL-CIO and some of its affiliates have for years been used by the CIA as a cover for its clandestine operations abroad to further the aims of American imperialism in Africa, British Guiana, the Dominican Republic, Southeast Asia and wherever else labor was needed by the CIA.

It is, therefore, not surprising that many young Americans have felt totally alienated from the labor movement. In the thirties many like them found in the labor movement a natural outlet for their ideals. When the workers asked in song *Which Side Are You On?* they responded that they were with organized labor. Today the same question most often brings an entirely opposite response. It does no good to remind them of labor's heritage of brave struggles and militant traditions. What are today's realities, they ask, and in the face of a labor movement increasingly at odds with its finest traditions, a movement which even after repeated pledges to organize the unorganized, represents only about a quarter of the organizable work force, and is failing to maintain this modest ratio as the labor force grows, how, they repeat, is it possible to regard organized labor as anything but an impediment in the move to achieve a better and more peaceful world?

Yet it would be well for them to understand that precisely this was being said by many liberals about the labor movement in the 1920's when it seemed that the prospect for changing the well entrenched, conservative craft character of the AFL and its indifference to the organization of the unskilled and semi-skilled, was remote. But even in a labor movement dominated by backward-looking traditionalists there existed, inside and outside of the AFL, a small nucleus of progressive and radical trade unionists who challenged the prevailing pattern. This progressive and radical goad helped, in part, to produce the great organizational achievements of the thirties. They would do well, too, to remember the struggle conducted some 35 years ago by the progressive forces in the labor movement for unemployment insurance in the face of the bitter opposition of the AFL leadership to the needs of millions of unemployed workers, including the members of the Federation, and their constant refrain that even starvation was better than the dole. But an AFL Committee for Unemployment Insurance came into being, and within a comparatively short period, hundreds of local unions throughout the country had endorsed it and committees were established in many centers of the labor movement forcing the AFL leadership reluctantly to endorse unemployment insurance, and leading to the establishment of the Unemployment Insurance Law.

What we are seeing today on many fronts in the labor movement, is a somewhat similar development as that which took place in the late twenties and thirties. The war in Vietnam has been a major factor in this development, but this, too, did not immediately make its influence felt in the labor movement. The upsurge of widespread opposition to the war in labor's ranks as it spilled over into Cambodia, is the product, in large measure, of earlier, if smaller, opposition to the war in Vietnam when the labor movement, in the main, supported the war. Yet no one reading recent books on the labor movement would ever know of the existence of these earlier labor protests against the war in Vietnam. In his *American Labor and United States Foreign Policy,* published in 1969, Ronald Radosh devotes six pages to

Vietnam, but finds no room for mention of the National Labor Leadership Assembly for Peace in November 1967, and leaves the reader with the clear impression that organized labor as a whole supported the war in Vietnam down to the time the book was completed.

A serious challenge is under way against the policies of the traditional labor leadership on many fronts and the war in Indochina is related to all of them. Critics of the labor movement may argue that the conservative leadership can absorb these counter-currents quite comfortably. One critic saw the White House dinner for labor leaders at which President Nixon gave America's top 200 union officials the unusual honor of dining with him, Mrs. Nixon and the Cabinet members and their wives, to be joined by 6,000 labor employees and their families for a military pageant, as "the final burial for what was a movement for progress. Movement gone: we now have the stagnation of the soul."[1] But after the election of 1970 was over, the *Wall Street Journal,* noting the election in working-class districts of many critics of the Nixon policies in Indochina, commented: "It must be clear now that having union leaders to dinners isn't going to capture labor's vote."[2]

No one should underestimate the difficulties that lie ahead for any effort to alter the role played by the dominant leadership of large sections of the American labor movement as uncritical supporters of the aims and purposes of U.S. foreign policy. But it is still true that there exists a mounting opposition in the trade unions to this conservative labor leadership and that this is, in many ways, part of the rising opposition in this country to American imperialism, the black liberation movement, and the rebellion of the youth. It is not unlikely as the wave of dissent with labor's traditional policies continues and increases, it will bring about a fundamental change in these policies, and, along with it, as part of the mass peace movement in this country, in alliance with students and other people's forces, bring an end to what the Labor Committee of the Detroit Coalition to End the War Now correctly described as "this disastrous, costly and racist war."

REFERENCE NOTES

1. INTRODUCTION

1. *Labor Voice for Peace,* Jan. 1968, p. 11.

2. Philip S. Foner, *History of the Labor Movement in the United States,* vol. II, New York, 1955, pp. 414–39; William George Whittaker, "Samuel Gompers, Anti-Imperialist," *Pacific Historical Review,* vol. XXXVIII, Nov. 1969, pp. 429–45.

3. V. I. Lenin, *Imperialism, the Highest Stage of Capitalism,* New York, 1939, p. 110. For discussions of American neo-colonialism, *see* Victor Perlo, *American Imperialism,* New York, 1951 and William J. Pomeroy, *American Neo-Colonialism: Its Emergence in the Philippines and Asia,* New York, 1970.

4. *The American Labor Year Book, 1916,* New York, 1916, pp. 128, 234, 236, 239; *The Public,* July 7, 1916.

5. Ronald Radosh, *American Labor and United States Foreign Policy,* New York, 1969, p. 8.

6. *Ibid.,* pp. 73–122; Philip S. Foner, *The Bolshevik Revolution: Its Impact on American Radicals, Liberals, and Labor,* New York, 1967, pp. 35–41.

7. *The American Labor Yearbook, 1927,* New York, 1928, pp. 226–28; *American Federationist,* Dec. 1933, p. 213.

8. Radosh, *op. cit.,* p. 355; *Labor and the War: Labor Fact Book 6,* New York, 1943, pp. 187–93; *Proceedings of the Constitutional Convention of the Congress of Industrial Organizations, 1938,* pp. 11–12.

9. Richard O. Boyer and Herbert M. Morais, *Labor's Untold Story,* New York, 1970, pp. 340–60; Art Preis, *Labor's Giant Step: Twenty Years of the CIO,* New York, 1964, p. 355; Radosh, *op. cit.,* p. 449.

10. *New York Times,* Nov. 2–4, 1949; Robert Bendiner, "Surgery in the CIO," *The Nation,* Nov. 12, 1949, p. 459.

11. New York *Herald Tribune,* Jan. 29, March 24, 1950; New York *Compass,* Feb. 1, 1950.

12. *The Nation,* Dec. 10, 1955, p. 509.

13. Arthur J. Goldberg, *AFL-CIO: Labor United,* New York, 1956, pp. 209–11; John P. Windmuller, "Foreign Affairs and the AFL-CIO," *Industrial and Labor Relations Review,* Vol. IX, April 1956, p. 427; *The Nation,* Dec. 10, 1955, p. 508.

14. *New York Times,* May 23, 1966.

15. *See* Philip Reno, "The Ordeal of British Guiana," *Monthly Review,* July-August, 1964, pp. 17–19; Stanley Meisler, "Dubious Role of AFL-CIO Meddling in Latin

America," *The Nation,* Feb. 10, 1965, pp. 133–38; Sidney Lens, "Lovestone Diplomacy," *The Nation,* July 5, 1965, p. 14; Dan Kurzman in Washington *Post,* Jan. 2, 1966.

16. Sidney Lens, "Labor Between Bread and Revolution," *The Nation,* Sept. 19, 1966, p. 251; Harry Bernstein, "AFL-CIO Unit Accused of 'Snooping' Abroad," Los Angeles *Times,* May 22, 1966; Neil Sheehan, "CIA Men Aided in Strikes in Guiana," *New York Times,* Feb. 23, 1967; Richard Dudman, "Agent Meany," *The New Republic,* May 3, 1969, pp. 13–16; Susane Bodenheimer, "The AFL-CIO in Latin America: The Dominican Republic—A Case Study," *Viet-Report,* Sept.-Oct. 1967, pp. 17–19; Thomas W. Braden, "I'm Glad the CIA is 'Immoral,' " *The Saturday Evening Post,* May 20, 1967, pp. 10–12.

The three most important books exposing the connections between the AFL-CIO and the CIA are: George Morris, *CIA and American Labor: The Subversion of the AFL-CIO's Foreign Policy,* New York, 1967; Serafino Romualdi, *Presidents and Peons: Recollections of a Labor Ambassador in Latin America,* New York, 1967, and Ronald Radosh, *American Labor and United States Foreign Policy,* New York, 1969. George Morris, whose book was the first to be published, had already exposed these connections in the *Daily Worker* of which he was the long-time labor editor.

2. LABOR BEGINS TO MOVE

1. *New York Times,* Jan. 18, 1961.

2. Fred Cook, "Juggernaut: The Warfare State," *The Nation,* Oct. 28, 1961, pp. 43–48.

3. *See* Joseph C. Goulden, *Truth is the First Casualty,* New York, 1969.

4. John P. Windmuller, "The Foreign Policy Conflict in American Labor," *Political Science Quarterly,* vol. LXXXII, June 1967, pp. 232–33.

5. *American Federationist,* Oct. 1962, pp. 12–22.

6. *I.U.D. Digest,* Fall 1962, p. 24.

7. *The Nation,* Oct. 13, 1962, p. 212.

8. Webster Schott, "The Teach-In: New Forum for Reason," *The Nation,* May 31, 1965, pp. 575–79; Christopher Lasch, "New Curriculum for Teach-Ins," *ibid.,* Oct. 18, 1965, pp. 239–41.

9. *Ibid.,* May 27, 1965, p. 573.

10. *New York Times,* Washington *Post,* April 18, 1965; *The Nation,* June 10, 1965, pp. 657–58.

11. Copy of telegram in archives of Local 1199.

12. *The Worker,* June 6, 1965.

13. *New York Times,* Nov. 12, 1965; New York *Post,* Dec. 12, 1965.

14. *Proceedings of the Sixth Annual Convention of the AFL-CIO, 1965,* pp. 65, 112–16.

15. *New York Times,* Dec. 11, 15, 1965; B. J. Widick, "AFL-CIO Convention: Strong Arm of the Status Quo," *The Nation,* Dec. 27, 1965, p. 516.

16. *New York Times,* Dec. 15, 1965.

17. *Ibid.,* Dec. 16, 1965.

18. Windmuller, *op. cit.,* pp. 218–19.

19. *New York Times,* Dec. 16, 1965.

20. George Morris, *CIA and American Labor,* p. 131; Paul E. Sultan, *The Disenchanted Unionist,* New York, 1963, p. 173.

21. The discussion of the Trade Union Division of SANE is based on materials in the Archives of the Division, Local 1199 headquarters. *See* also New York *Post,* May 11, 1966 and Anne P. Draper, "Unions and the War in Vietnam," *New Politics,* Summer 1966, pp. 8–12.

22. Windmuller, *op. cit.,* pp. 219–20; *New York Times,* Nov. 15, 1966.

23. Radosh, *op. cit.,* p. 445.

24. Mimeographed statement issued by Trade Union Division of SANE, in the Archives of the Division, Local 1199 headquarters.

25. The discussion of the chapters in the Far West and Chicago is based on correspondence in the Archives of the Trade Union Division of SANE, Local 1199 headquarters. See also Los Angeles *Herald-Examiner,* Jan. 20, 1967.

3. LABOR ASSEMBLY FOR PEACE

1. New York *Daily News,* May 16, 1967; *New York Times,* May 16, 1967.

2. Moe Foner to A. N. "Nate" Sough, May 16, 1967; Moe Foner to Paul Perlin, May 17, 1967, Archives of the Trade Union Division of SANE, Local 1199 headquarters. *See also The Nation,* Oct. 9, 1967, p. 325.

3. The discussion of the National Labor Leadership Assembly for Peace is based on *Labor Voice for Peace,* Jan. 1968; B. J. Widick, "Labor Meets for Peace," *The Nation,* Nov. 27, 1967, pp. 561–63; William J. Abbott, "Not All of Labor Agrees with Meany," *The New Republic,* Nov. 25, 1967, pp. 15–16; *New York Times,* Nov. 12–14, 1967; Chicago *Sun,* Nov. 13–15, 1967; Harvey O'Connor, "Harbinger of A New Day?" *Monthly Review,* Jan. 1968, pp. 27–30.

4. Several press comments are reprinted in *Labor's Voice for Peace,* Jan. 1968. *See also The Nation,* Nov. 27, 1967, p. 549.

5. Los Angeles *Times,* Dec. 10, 1967; Washington *Post, New York Times,* New York *Post,* Dec. 11–14, 1967; B. J. Widick, "Look at Bal Harbour: Meany's Wooden Soldiers," *The Nation,* Jan. 1, 1968, pp. 6–8; *Proceedings, AFL-CIO Convention,* 1968, pp. 230–62.

6. *Labor Voice for Peace,* April 1968.

7. *Labor Voice for Peace,* Jan. and April 1968.

8. *Ibid.; The Nation,* Jan. 29, 1968, p. 132.

9. *New York Times,* March 13, 1968; copy of telegram in Archives of National Labor Leadership Assembly for Peace, Local 1199 headquarters.

10. San Francisco *Examiner,* May 20, 1968; *Daily World,* Aug. 3, 1968.

11. Moe Foner to Patrick E. Gorman, Jan. 30, 1968, Archives of National Labor Leadership Assembly for Peace, Local 1199 headquarters.

12. *The Nation,* Nov. 27, 1967, p. 562.

13. *Labor Voice for Peace,* April 1968; *The Nation,* March 11, 1968, p. 342.

14. *The Nation,* April 8, 1968, p. 464.

15. *Ibid.,* March 18, 1968, p. 369; April 29, 1968, p. 556; June 17, 1968, p. 783.

16. *New York Times,* Aug. 15–17, 1968.

17. *Ibid.,* Sept. 12, 1968.

4. DIVISION DEEPENS

1. B. J. Widick, "ALA: New Voice of Labor," *The Nation,* June 16, 1968, pp. 758–60.

2. *New York Times,* Dec. 7, 1968.

3. A. Bilik, "Labor Against Itself: The Alienated Rank and File," *The Nation,* Nov. 17, 1969, pp. 527–30.

4. Copy of leaflet in author's possession.

5. Al Richmond, "Workers Against the War," *Ramparts,* Sept., 1970, p. 31.

6. Leaflet entitled, "Nixon Brings the War Home," in author's possession; *Labor Today,* March-April 1970.

7. *New York Times,* Oct. 16, 1969; New York *Post,* Oct. 16–17, 1969; Detroit *Free Press,* Oct. 16, 1969; Los Angeles *Times,* Oct. 16, 1969; *1199 Drug & Hospital News,* Nov. 1969.

8. *New York Times,* Oct. 3, 1969.

9. Copy of eight-page leaflet in author's possession.

10. *Labor Today,* March-April 1970, p. 5; "Labor and Nov. 15," *International Socialist,* Dec. 1969.

11. *Missouri Teamster,* January, February, 1970; St. Louis *Post-Dispatch,* Feb. 18, 1970.

12. New York *Daily News,* March 28, 1970; *New York Times,* May 7, 1970.

13. Copy of telegram in author's possession.

14. *Daily World,* April 16, 1970.

15. *New York Times,* April 12, 1970.

16. *Dissent,* May-June 1970, pp. 10–15.

5. CAMBODIA: INITIAL RESPONSE

1. *The New Republic,* May 16, 1970, p. 8.

2. Morris, *CIA and American Labor,* p. 154.

3. Detroit *Free Press,* May 2, 1970; copy of telegram released by General Council of District 65 in author's possession.

4. *UAW President Walter Reuther's Last Public Statement.* Four-page leaflet issued by UAW Education Department.

5. Copy of statement by UE General Executive Board, May 7, 1970, in author's possession.

6. Copy of resolution adopted by the 18th international convention of the American Federation of State, County and Municipal Employees, AFL-CIO, in author's possession.

7. *Daily World,* May 8, 9, 1970; copy of resolution adopted by Central Labor Council of Alameda, California, in author's possession; Richmond, "Workers Against the War," *Ramparts,* Sept., 1970, pp. 28–29.

8. *New York Times,* May 9–11, 1970; *Wall Street Journal,* May 10–12, 1970.

9. *New York Times,* May 10–12, 1970; New York *Post,* May 10, 12–14, 1970; *Wall Street Journal,* May 12, 1970; Fred J. Cook, "Hard Hats: The Rampaging Patriots," *The Nation,* June 15, 1970, pp. 712–13.

10. St. Louis *Post Dispatch,* June 15, 1970.

11. *The New Yorker,* June 6, 1970; *New York Times,* May 27, 1970.

12. *New York Times,* May 12, 1970.

13. *Wall Street Journal,* May 11, 1970. *See also Time,* May 25, 1970, p. 21.

14. New York *Post,* May 15–20, 22–24, 1970; Cook, *op. cit.,* pp. 712–14.

15. *Scanlan's Monthly,* July, 1970; *New York Times,* July 22, 1970.

16. *New York Times,* May 12, 1970.

17. *Daily World,* May 13, 1970.

18. *Wall Street Journal,* May 19, 1970.

19. *New York Times,* Nov. 12, 1969.

20. *Ibid.,* March 24, 1970.

21. *Time,* Aug. 17, 1970, p. 62.

22. New York *Post,* May 21, 1970.

23. *Time,* May 25, 1970, p. 21; *Guardian,* May 30, 1970.

24. *New York Times,* July 26, 1970.

25. Jimmy Breslin, "One Way to End the War," *New York,* June 22, 1970, p. 28.

26. *New York Times,* June 18, 1970.

27. *Daily World,* June 19, 1970.

6. LABOR-STUDENT ALLIANCES

1. Washington *Post,* May 11, 1970; *District 65 News,* June 1970.

2. Copy of press release of editorial in author's possession. *See also The Butcher Workman,* June-July 1970.

3. *1199 Drug & Hospital News,* June 1970.

4. *New York Times,* May 20, 1970.

5. *Daily World,* May 20, 1970.

6. New York *Post,* May 20, 21, 1970.

7. *New York Times,* May 22, 1970; Cook, *op. cit.,* p. 718.

8. *New York Times,* May 23, 24, 25, 1970.

9. St. Paul *Union Advocate,* May 21, 1970.

10. *Labor,* May 26, 1970.

11. Copy of News Release by UAW International Executive Board, May 25, 1970, in author's possession.

12. *Keynote Address of Jacob S. Potofsky, General President, 27th biennial convention, Amalgamated Clothing Workers of America, AFL-CIO, CLC, Atlantic City, New Jersey, May 25, 1970,* pp. 9–16.

13. *New York Times,* May 25, 1970; New York *Post,* May 25, 1970.

14. *New York Times,* May 25, 1970.

15. Chicago *Daily News,* May 16, 1970; Detroit *Free Press,* Nov. 16, 1970.

16. *Labor Today,* March-April, May-June, 1970; *Minneapolis Labor Review,* May 28, 1970.

17. *New York Times,* June 18, July 27, 1970; *1199 Drug & Hospital News,* July 1970.

18. Copy of President Leonard Woodcock's testimony before the Joint Economic Committee of Congress furnished by the UAW Education Department, in author's possession.

19. The proceedings of the National Rank and File Action Conference are published in a special issue of *Labor Today,* July-August 1970. Good coverage may also be found in the *Daily World,* June 27–30, July 11, 1970. For a critical view of the conference, *see* the article by David Moberg in *Guardian,* July 4, 1970, p. 7.

20. *Daily World,* Aug. 6, 1970.

21. *New York Times,* Aug. 31, 1970; *Time,* Sept. 14, 1970, p. 16; *Daily World,* Aug. 25, 1970.

22. *Detroit News,* May 28, 1970.

23. *Wall Street Journal,* Sept. 14, 1970; Washington *Post,* Sept. 16, 1970; *Daily World,* Sept. 16, 1970.

24. *New York Times,* Aug. 31, 1970.

25. *Ibid.,* Sept. 27, 1970; *Daily World,* Sept. 25, 29, 30, 1970.

26. FLM Joint Board *Tempo,* July 1970.

7. CONCLUSION

1. Martin Wolfson in letter to New York *Post,* Sept. 11, 1970.

2. *Wall Street Journal,* Nov. 12, 1970.

ABOUT THE AUTHOR

DR. PHILIP S. FONER, Professor of History at Lincoln University, Pennsylvania, is best known for his original studies of the labor movement in the United States and the history of the Afro-American freedom struggle. The first four volumes of his *History of the Labor Movement in the United States* have been widely acclaimed as a valuable contribution and an indispensable source for all interested in the subject. His four-volume *The Life and Writings of Frederick Douglass* has been called "a monumental piece of historical scholarship" (Professor Alain Locke). He is the author of many shorter studies and monographs on labor and related themes, as well as essays and articles in scholarly and labor journals, and lectures widely. He thus brings to the present book a rich background of scholarship and experience.